2-18-2019

For Ed Mason, fellow writer.
Keep writing!

Carol Purroy

YOUR LEGACY

The stories of your life

by

Carol Purroy, M.A.

A-Z Publishing

TABLE OF CONTENTS

PREFACE

Every time an elder dies a library is lost.

Proverb

That says it all.

All our lives we're told, "You can't take it with you." But think about it and you'll realize what a lot you *will* take with you.

You'll take with you everything you've learned, everything you've experienced, everything you've figured out or discovered over the course of your life.

You'll take with you your skills and talents, your personal history and your family's history.

You'll take with you your knowledge of your era.

You'll take with you your personality, your character, your sense of humor, your values . . . your uniqueness.

Think about all your ancestors took with them – in most cases, their entire "libraries." But wouldn't you love to know about your grandparents and great-grandparents and even your more distant ancestors: their dreams, their proudest accomplishments.

Wouldn't you like to know how they endured their hardships and overcame obstacles?

Wouldn't you like to know how and why they made their life-altering decisions?

Wouldn't you *love* to know their love stories?

And how they felt about and responded to the events and issues of their day?

Wouldn't it be great to have a window into what made them laugh, what made them cry . . . what made them "tick."

Psychologists tell us that a large part of our sense of Self – our identity -- comes from knowing about our heritage. Our ancestors are part of us. We have their DNA. A lot of who we are is because of them. Wouldn't it be wonderful if we could connect with them through their stories, letters, essays, etc., and learn what we have in common with them?

They may have taken their "libraries" with them, but you don't have to. There's still time for you to create your legacy. It may be the most important thing you'll ever write, even more important than your Last Will & Testament, which is, after all, only about money and material things.

It's possible that the most important thing you can leave behind is your "library" – the story of YOU. It's your truest legacy.

INTRODUCTION

My parents died too soon. I realize that's true of everyone's parents, but I was just a child when mine passed on, and I hadn't even thought about getting their stories. It's left a big hole in my life. I *want* to know about my mom and dad, but they're gone and there's no one I can ask. There are so many things I don't know. I don't know how they met and fell in love. I don't know what they enjoyed doing, other than dancing – I'm told they were terrific dancers. I know very little about their childhoods – their school years. I don't know about their dreams, their plans for the future. There's so much I can never know.

There are photographs of the two generations before me, for which I am grateful. But I'd like to know the stories that go with those faces. And I'd like to know more about earlier generations, those who lived before cameras existed, who are just names and dates on a genealogy chart. It's nice to know that much, but I wish I had their stories, too.

I wonder why my two sets of grandparents left their homelands (Denmark and Missouri, USA), their families and friends, and why they chose California's Central Valley in which to settle. I wonder what it was like for them when they arrived and settled in. Was it what they expected? How did they cope with being young and on their own in a strange land? How did they develop a support system? What did they do to survive -- both physically and emotionally?

I wish I had just a scrap of paper written by or about them, or some earlier ancestors, that would give me a glimpse into their lives.[1]

This project, first the classes and now the book, grew out of that sense of loss. I started teaching the Life Stories class in 1991 because I didn't want that to happen to others. I offered a forum through which seniors were encouraged to get their stories written. I hope each of you will pass on as much of yourselves as you can so your children and grandchildren, and *their* children and grandchildren, will know you.

Here's a sobering thought: if you have offspring you will someday be someone's distant ancestor. He/She/They will be thrilled to know about you . . . *if* you write your stories. Conversely, if you don't, they may feel the lack.

Whether you are writing your stories for family and friends or for a much broader audience, this book is for you.

---

1   Since the first printing of *Your Legacy* (formerly titled *Your Life Oughta Be A Book*) I've learned that a letter in which Grandpa Petersen proposed to Grandma exists. I now have a copy, which I treasure.

Planning to write is not writing.
Outlining a book is not writing.
Researching is not writing.
Talking to people about what you're doing,
none of that is writing.
Writing is writing.

E. L. Doctorow

YOUR LIFE OUGHT TO BE A BOOK

Your life ought to be a book, and boy, have you got stories to tell. You don't have to have been an astronaut, a bank robber, a movie star, or a "madam" to have stories worth writing about. Your life is exotic.

It's possible that you don't think of it as anything out of the ordinary. And maybe, for your time and place, it wasn't. But you're writing for future generations about what it was like to be a child, a teenager, a young adult, and even a mature adult in a time they can't even imagine. So far as they're concerned, it's like a visit to another planet.

You'll be telling them what your school days, your profession, your hometown and family were like. You'll tell about kitchen appliances and work implements and toys that will amaze and amuse them. You'll write about the pastimes and adventures of a bygone time. You'll clue them in on the fads and fancies of your era. *That's* exotic!

You'll place historic events in a very personal light and, by doing so, allow your readers to learn things that aren't in the history books.

When history books tell about a war, for example, we learn the goals of both sides, the names of the top generals, the dates and locations of the major battles, and which side won. *(Yawn.)*

However, by placing individuals and families in those events and bringing to light their personalities, goals, thoughts, emotions, experiences, their triumphs and tragedies, we not only learn a lot about that war, we also find ourselves caring about its events and their outcome, as well as the characters themselves.

If you're like me, when you get to "know" the people involved, you care about them. You live vicariously through them. You weep when they're sad, smile when they're happy, laugh out loud at their foibles. You'll teach your readers about your era, its events and the people who lived through them in a way that really grabs them. You'll get them involved in a very personal historical account -- yours.

What were your experiences of your war eras? WWII? The Korean War? The Vietnam War? The Persian Gulf War? The Iraq and/or Afghanistan War? Whether you were in the trenches, dodging bullets – or dodging the draft, or protesting your country's involvement, or maybe volunteering at the USO, serving dough-nuts and playing pingpong with the troops -- it affected your life and influenced you.

Where were you and what were you doing on "9/11," when the World Trade Center and the Pentagon were attacked by hijacked airplanes? What were your thoughts and emotions as you watched it happen or learned about it? What effect did it have on you?

And what about the other major social- and culture-changing periods of your lifetime? How have you and your life changed because of them?

How about the inventions and innovations of your lifetime? What impact has any of them had on your life? How? Why?

Boy, have you got stories to tell.

HISTORY'S MYSTERIES

Remember that old philosophical question, "If a tree falls in the forest and there's no one there to hear it, does it make a sound?"

How about this one: "If you lived on this planet but no one here knows anything about you, who gives a good 'Gee Whiz'?"

Oh, some people care . . . now. But a generation or two into the future, who will know? Or care? Fifty or a hundred years from now, you'll just be one of history's mysteries, having faded into anonymity and obscurity . . . unless you write your stories.

Marco Polo is a name familiar to most of us. But who was he? He was a 13th century teenager from Venice, Italy who tagged along with a group of tradesmen on a trip to China. Why do we know about him but not the others who went before, with, or after him? Because he wrote his story.

He told of his incredible adventures and discoveries, inform- ing current (13th century) and future generations about himself, his era and his discoveries. The others did not. This adolescent who went along for the ride stole their thunder; he's the one we know about. Perhaps the adults he accompanied had great influence at the time but, because they didn't write their stories, they are just a footnote in history – an anonymous, obscure footnote.

Don't be like them. And don't be like that tree, falling silently in the forest.

Make some noise!

Exclaim yourself!

Pronounce yourself!

Celebrate your life!

Your readers, whoever they may be, want to know you – your character, your values, your quirks, your passions, your philosophy, your sense of humor, your accomplishments, your philanthropies, your adventures and *mis*adventures, your adversities, your adversaries, your struggles, your complexities, what makes you tick, what interests you, what excites you, who you fell in love with, how you chose your career(s), why you moved from one part of the world to another, what you have learned about life, *et cetera.*

Like Marco Polo, leave a record of your life and times for current and future generations.

(Of course, you may want parts of your history to remain a mystery. That's okay. You're entitled.)

WONDER IF YOU'RE UP TO IT?

You may look upon the task of writing your life stories with dread or even horror. Perhaps you don't know where to begin or how to go about it. You will, no doubt, want to write stories or a book that people will enjoy reading; a page-turner they won't be able to put down.

You will want to write it in such a way that people will enjoy reading it, not just because they know and love you, but because it's a good read on its own merits. But you may wonder if you're up to it.

Chances are you're not a writer, or haven't been up 'til now. Maybe you're not the world's best speller and your grammar ain't exactly the Queen's English. Your vocabulary may not be the equal of a Fullbright Scholar's.

No matter. Help is at hand. The purpose of this book is to make the job of telling your stories easier. But equally important, it is to help you create a finished product that will captivate and intrigue your readers. In the pages that follow, you'll find tips on how to accomplish that.

WHO IN (THEIR) RIGHT MIND WRITES AN AUTOBIOGRAPHY?

Fortunately, an autobiography or memoir is not one of those documents that usually begins, "Being of sound mind, I . . ." Memoir writing has no such requirement, so go for it regardless of your state of mind.

More and more people are now thinking about writing their life stories, and actually doing it. Whether they're in their right mind matters not a whit. But since they are contemplating it and doing it, many are finding that they could use a little help and encouragement.

This book's appeal is probably mostly to people in their later years, simply because that group now has time to sit down, cogitate, reflect, and write. Also, members of this group have reached the point in life at which they can look back and reflect, placing things in perspective and trying to make some sense out of it. I call it the "What's it all about, Alfie?-syndrome."

They are discovering that they want to pass on to others what they have spent a lifetime learning. They want to leave something meaningful behind. And let's face it, most of us will never have a monument erected or an airport named in our honor, so memoir is the thing.

They may be seeking a new purpose, or simply a purposeful way to fill their time, their formal careers having ended. Writing the stories of their lives fills the bill.

They are often encouraged (nagged) by their kids and grandkids to tell their stories. And those kids and grandkids really do want to know about you, so don't be recalcitrant. Just do it. For them.

However, people of all ages, like our 13th century teenager can and should be recording their life experiences, as well as their thoughts and emotions about the events of their lives. (We tend to forget that day-by-day events are history in the making.) This may be done in letters to a good friend, a diary or journal. It can be newspaper clippings or favorite books with notes scribbled in the margins. These will prove invaluable later on when you want to sit down and write your own history.

In this little book is a list of topics to help spark ideas. It also includes a variety of approaches to writing your own stories. There are helpful hints on making it less a dry-as-dust history lesson and more a juicy tale of flesh and blood people.

This book is for all autobiographers: those who simply want to write bits and pieces as well as those who will pen full-fledged books, novels or plays based on pieces of their lives, and everyone in between. Do not be intimidated, thinking you must write volumes. To qualify as an autobiographer or memoirist you need only write something – anything – about your own life and/or your family's.

Your Life Oughta Be A Book is for memoirists at all levels.

I invite you to take from it what you need, whatever fits. If parts of it do not apply to you or your project, simply discard them. In your stories you want your uniqueness to come through, so there are no hard and fast rules.

Do not allow yourself to become stressed by writing your life stories. Let yourself have fun in the reminiscing and the telling of it.

What is needed for this task is for you to get into your *write mind* and don't give your *right mind* a second thought.

WHAT TO WRITE ABOUT

Writers sometimes get stuck or have a hard time getting started in the first place. The task of writing about one's life can seem overwhelming.

Starting on the next page is a partial list of suggested story topics. Not all will apply to everyone. It is offered only to introduce possible subjects for your memoirs. There is no suggestion that you try to incorporate all, or even most, of them.

Throughout this book are examples of a few of these topics, compiled from both published and unpublished autobiographies. From them you'll get an inkling of what is possible. They are entertaining and informative -- a good read. And they may give you ideas for your own stories.

While the list is quite long, it's only a fraction of the topics you could include in your life story. It's just to get you started thinking.

You may choose to write an entire story or anecdote on a single topic or merely mention it in passing.

TOPICS

• Recollections or legends about relatives: parents, siblings, grandparents, distant ancestors, etc., aunts, uncles, cousins.

• Your child(ren) and grandchild(ren): their births, infancies and childhoods. How each one is special.

• Adoptees: Your search for and/or discovery of your birth parent(s), or why you chose not to search for them.

• Your relationship with your parent(s), as a child or an adult.

• Your most heartwarming, terrifying or tragic memory.

• What you hoped your parents would never find out about, and what happened if they did.

• Your family's superstitions and/or customs.

• How illness was treated in your family.

• Health and accidents. Experiences with doctors and hospitals.

• Holidays: your family's, neighborhood's or culture's customs and traditions.

• How a family tradition started.

• Where you were and what you were doing when you felt most alive.

• Adventures, travels.

• Your enemy(ies).

• Your hero(es).

- Risks you took, or wish you had taken.
- Historical events. Where you were, what you were doing, how it impacted your life when:
  - A war began or ended.
  - An important person died.
  - A natural disaster struck (hurricane, earthquake, flood, fire, tornado, ice storm).
  - When an important event occurred.
- Memories of a socio-political movement.
- A turning point.
- Your romances. The love(s) of your life:
  - How you met
  - What attracted you
  - How you managed to get together
- Your heartbreaks.
- The most romantic moment of your life.
- Rites of passage -- coming of age rites.
- Sex education. Who taught you about sex? How?
- First date. First Kiss. First sexual experience.
- Your greatest disappointment.
- Challenges, obstacles you overcame -- or didn't.
- Your most bizarre or unusual experience.
- Your most courageous act.
- The thing you're most proud of.
- Things you wish you could change.
- "If I knew then what I know now . . ."
- Your mistakes and what you learned from them.

- Good friends. Important people.
- Jobs: the first, the worst, the best, the weirdest, the most fulfilling, the most fun, etc.
- How/why you chose your career(s), or it/they chose you.
- Your spiritual journey:
    - Your spiritual philosophy
    - How you got to where you are now spiritually
    - The impact it has had on your life.
    - An epiphany
- Best (or worst) advice you were given.
- Your politics:
    - Your political philosophy and/or affiliation
    - Your political/social activism
    - How you got to where you are now politically
- Your concerns, pursuits, missions, purpose.
- Disobedience, civil or uncivil.
- Pets.
- "As my (e.g: grandma) used to say . . . "
- How your parents (or surrogates) raised you: what was important to them. How you raised (or will raise) your children differently, or the same.
- How you were taught values.
- How you were named.
- The origin of your nickname.
- A humiliation or embarrassment.
- Your special talents, skills, attributes.
- Clubs, organizations you belong(ed) to.

• The ironies of your life.

• The smartest or dumbest thing you've ever done.

• Wealth and/or poverty in your life.

• Food, special meals, recipes.

• Fragrances, aromas that elicit memories.

• Music, songs, concerts, instruments, dancing.

• Radio & TV shows.

• Movies and movie stars.

• Fads.

• Toys.

• Cars.

• Clothes, shoes, hats.

• Furniture.

• Jewelry.

• Inventions or innovations.

• Sports.

• What it was like being a child in your era; who you were as a child:

    • What you enjoyed doing

    • How you spent summer days

    • School days

    • Dreams, fantasies.

    • Friends

    • Games you played; songs you sang.

    • Artifacts of the period.

• What it was like being a teenager in your era. (See above list.)

• Who you were as a young adult:

- Leaving home
- College/University days
- Military duty
- Relationships
- Jobs
- Dreams, goals, fantasies, plans for the future.
- An unforgettable character. Someone who influenced you.
- Being maligned or treated/judged unfairly.
- Abuses, tortures you endured.
- The nicest/worst thing anyone's ever done for/to you.
- The best/worst day of your life.
- The best gift (tangible or intangible) anyone ever gave you.
- Hobbies. Collections.
- Your brush with celebrity.
- A brush with death. A near-death experience.
- Miracles, angels, divine intervention.
- Kismet - Destiny - Fate. Serendipity, Synchronicity.
- A supernatural or paranormal experience:
    - Visits/Messages from beyond the grave
    - Ghosts
    - "Invisible friends"
    - An out-of-body experience.
    - Extraterrestrial sightings, experiences.
- Loss, grief, bereavement, healing.
- Something you cannot forgive of another.
- Something you'd like to be forgiven for.
- Your life's mission or purpose.

• How life turned out different than you expected.
• Regrets:
  • What you did that you wish you hadn't.
  • What you didn't do that you wish you had.
• The biggest lie you ever told . . . and the consequences.
• Your health (medical) history, including whatever you know about your ancestors' health history. (This could be part of a section on genealogy. While it is probably not the most exciting to your general audience, it is vital to your descendants.)

The possibilities are infinite. I'm sure you can add plenty of your own topics to this list.

In the next section are further suggestions on where to get ideas to write about. Write about whatever comes to mind. The important thing is to get going and *just do it.*

WHERE TO GET IDEAS

At any point in writing your life stories you may experience a bit of a slowdown. Following are some sure-fire resources to spur you on:

• Family Albums. You'll see photographs of yourself, your family and friends, of holidays, celebrations, rites of passage, ceremonies, vacations, etc., and memories will come in a deluge. Every picture has a story.

• Scrapbooks. Every item in a scrapbook was placed there to remind you at some future time about the good times you had: special events, vacations, holidays, *et cetera*. So every page is filled with stories for you to write.

• Music. As you listen to music from your past, certain pieces will remind you of another time -- a romantic time, a poignant time, a triumphant time, a time of terror, a time of sadness. Music has the power to transport us through time and space better than almost anything else.

• A Reunion. As you see and talk with old friends, colleagues and relatives, you'll be inundated with memories, some of which you may want to write about. Chances are, you'll also learn new information or added tidbits that may be worthy of inclusion in your memoirs.

• Fragrance, Aroma, Scent. Fragrance is the most powerful memory jogger. Aromas of food and flowers -- scents reminiscent of another time and place -- bring back memories, sensations and emotions.

• Movies & TV Shows. Something in a movie or TV show, especially period pieces, may remind us of something in our history: a situation, a relationship, an artifact, toy, old car or airplane, a piece of furniture or clothing, or even a painting on the wall in the film.

• Household items: Furniture, books, china, silver, *objets d'art,* toys, jewelry. Look around your house at the furniture and knickknacks. Poke around in the attic, basement, cedar chest, china cabinet, bookcase, jewelry box. You're bound to find several items with stories.

• Cookbooks, Recipe Boxes. You'll recall special meals, special occasions and special people as you go through your cookbooks and recipe files. Many of our pleasantest (and some of our awfulest) memories are associated with food and cooking.

Other People's Life Stories. Read other people's biographies and autobiographies and listen to others' life stories. You'll think of incidents, people or places that you'll want to write about. They're great memory joggers.

You never know where inspiration will come from, so in addition to checking through the "What to Write About" list and the "Where To Get Ideas" resources from time to time, I urge you to keep your antennæ receptive and allow yourself to reminisce wherever you go.

For example, my sister Pat and I attended a cousin's funeral and encryptment in a mausoleum. In the middle of the ceremony I poked Pat with my elbow and whispered, "Does this place remind you of anything?" She nodded and whispered back. Sure enough, her association was the same as mine, based on a very peculiar ritual in our childhood. It got me thinking and I realized it was an anecdote I should write up. (See "A Bizarre Ritual.")

*When I have trouble writing, I step outside my
studio into the garden and pull weeds until my mind clears.
I find weeding to be the best therapy there is for writer's block.*
Irving Stone

Writing Activity #1

Look through a photo album or scrapbook for a story idea.

Pretend you're showing the album to someone -- a grandchild, for instance. As you come to a photo or memento that brings back memories, you'll want to tell him or her about it:

- What was going on at that time
- What you remember about the day (or event) that photo was taken
- What other associations you have regarding it

That's your story. Write it.

Have fun!

GET THEIR ATTENTION

How do you get your readers to continue past the opening sentence? How do you get them to want to enter into your story and experience it with you? How do you get them hooked?

You start off with a bang!

The first two or three sentences are all important to your story. Its beginning should elicit three or more questions in your readers' minds.

Below are a few from my memoir, *That's Life*, each followed by three questions that might be elicited:

• "The thing that terrified me most was not the bogeyman or

imaginary monsters under my bed."

What questions does that story opening elicit for you? Possible questions:

What was it that terrified her?

Was it animal or human? Or something else?

What did it do that terrified her so?

• "Sometimes our dreams betray us."

What was her dream?

How did it betray her?

What went wrong?

• "Now single, with no husband to tell me what I could or couldn't do, I was feeling frivolous."

What did she want to do?

What did she consider "daring and different?" "Frivolous?"

What was the outcome?

• "Every time I convince myself it was just a figment of my imagination, something happens to jar myself out of my complacency."

What was it -- that "figment of (her) imagination?"

What happened to jar her out of her "complacency?"

And then what happened, when she again thought it might be real?

And one final one:

• "The call every parent fears came in the middle of the night."

Who's calling?

What news did she receive?

How did she respond?

Youngest sons Alexs stabbing.

You get the idea. Wherever possible you want to lead off with an intriguing statement.

Although I've put "Start off With a Bang" up front in this book, it's generally something that I give my attention to after I've finished writing the story. I just want you to be thinking about it. You can always play around with the opening later and make it more intriguing.

Writing Activity #2

Write about an event in your life between the ages of 6 and 12.

• This is a time period is rich with memories . . . and stories. It covers your entire elementary school experience, so there are the schoolyard bullies, the sweet kids, the "best friend," your teachers, music lessons, baseball teams, Boy/Girl Scouts, church/temple/mosque, games, toys, hobbies, activities, radio/TV shows, movies, your parents and siblings, plus whatever was going on in the world at that time. (For me, World War II was in the background, so a lot of my kid stories have that association.)

• Let your mind drift until you remember something that happened during that time.

• Write about it.

Have fun!

FOOD AS A STORY STARTER

It's a fact that many of us cook, and all of us eat. Food is a constant in our lives, and we all have a favorite food or recipe. All of us have memories associated with food, from snatching a pre-dinner taste in Grandma's kitchen to perhaps an elegant dinner in a posh restaurant or on an ocean liner. Maybe you had a memorable dinner in a far-off land, or learned to love a particular dish you first tasted on your travels.

Food is a terrific memory jogger. A dish or recipe may be the topic of your story. Or it could be the trigger that reminds you of an event or adventure, the food mentioned as part of the story.

The following anecdote was written by Lawrence Green of

Reno, NV:

The Best Meal I Ever Had

If you have ever reflected on the topic above you may have had some trouble identifying your choice. I did not. I know the answer.

In my 20-plus years in the Air Force, I dined in many places: Paris, London, New York, New Orleans, San Francisco, Honolulu, Tokyo, Singapore, Saigon and Sydney, to drop a few. The best meal I ever had did not occur at any of those. Rather, it was a place you may never have heard of -- Thule AFB, Greenland, 600 miles north of the Arctic Circle, the farthest north in the world.

As a young fighter pilot I was part of our first line of defense against a Russian attack coming over The Pole in 1953, at the height of the Cold War. Temperatures ranged from 25° above to 55° below 0°.

The Air Force may put you in harm's way, but they do want you to survive. I had been to desert survival school, jungle survival school, mountain survival school, and now I was going to ice cap survival school.

After a half-day "training," ten of us were taken out to the Arctic ice cap and spaced a good distance apart, with only the equipment we brought in -- a backpack parachute and a 15 x 15" seat pack. In it was everything needed to survive few days, including an ice saw. Each of us was to construct an igloo, then sit tight. They would pick us up in 72 hours.

As it happened, a helluva storm blew in and they couldn't come get us. They didn't show up. And they didn't show up. And they didn't show up. Finally, by the time they got there, I had consumed all my provisions.

And I was getting hungry.

I was taken by snowcat to a quonset hut -- a warm, cozy quonset hut. Talk about ambience! The other nine were rescued too, so I was in the company of good friends. We were treated to breakfast.

Each of us got two stale do-nuts and two ultra-cold Coors beers.

It was definitely the best meal I ever had!

Here's a tidbit from my (autobiographical) cookbook. It accompanies a recipe I got from my good friend, Agnes Foo, many years ago:

Agnes hails from Shanghai, China. She's the mother of three boys, as I am. Across-the-street neighbors, we were sort of second-mothers to each other's kids. As they were growing up, her middle son, Patrick, did not like Chinese food, while my youngest, Alex, loved it.

Whenever Agnes was cooking Chinese food I'd get a phone call. "I'm cooking Chinese tonight. You wanna to trade kids?"

Alex went across the street to dine on exotic delicacies while Patrick came to our house for Macaroni & Cheese or Tuna Noodle Casserole, or whatever we were having, and everyone was happy.

I mentioned my cookbook earlier. This is a book of recipes

compiled over the years. I put it together for my sons and grand-daughter. I included a very brief memoir with many of the recipes. Sometimes it's just my recollection of the person who gave me the recipe, other times it's about a time that dish was served, and still others, it's about a tradition featuring that dish.

Following is the "memoir" accompanying the recipe for Orange Rolls:

These delicious rolls were a staple at our holiday dinners. I suspect the recipe goes back many, many generations, maybe all the way to my maternal ancestors in England. In our family, no holiday dinner was complete without them.

Back when the recipe and the tradition began, oranges were a rare and expensive delicacy for anyone not living in a warm, southern climate.

My mother told of her childhood Christmasses in Missouri. Each child in the family would get just one present. And each one's Christmas stocking would contain a few pieces of hard candy, some nuts, and an orange, this last a huge treat to be savored.

And then at Christmas dinner, these orange rolls would be the *piece d'resistance.*

In doing research for my cookbook, i.e., going through my recipe box and cookbooks, which were jammed with newspaper clippings and bits of paper on which recipes were scribbled, I was inundated with memories -- people I hadn't thought about in a long time but who meant so much to me; experiences and even whole eras I'd all but forgotten; dinners, parties, picnics, and holiday gatherings.

I encourage you to dig through your recipes and unearth your own memories, and write them down for your friends and offspring, and theirs.

Since *Your Legacy* was first published (as Your Life Oughta Be A Book), I've also written and published a children's historical novel set in 1946 (for ages 8 - 12) -- *Miss Rogers Stinks* -- in which a cookie recipe plays an important role. It's fiction, but was inspired by an event in my Fifth grade year.

It's available at: www.tinyurl.com/MissRogersStinks.

(p.s. That's my 5th grade self on the cover.)

Writing Activity #3

Write a story in which food plays a part.

• Search your memory banks to find a story about one of the following -- or use one of your own ideas:

  • The best meal I ever had.

  • The worst meal I ever had.

  • My most romantic meal.

  • My mom's best dish.

  • My dad, the cook.

  • The most exotic (or memorable) meal on my trip to

_____.

      • A camping trip: campfire cooking, etc.

  • Growing/picking/gathering your own food.

    • Being hungry.

  • A traditional holiday dish.

  • Grandma's kitchen.

  • Preserving homegrown food: canning, making jams,
      jellies, pickles, chutney, etc.

  • The first packaged foods, or cooking from scratch.

  • The most elegant place I've ever dined.

  • Potluck suppers, family gatherings, etc.

You have so many options for stories it will be difficult to pick just one. You may end up with a cookbook of your own (or your writing group's), or an anthology of stories and essays about food.

• Have fun!

THE BALLOON METHOD

Once you have decided upon a topic, where do you go from there? The Balloon Method is an excellent way of recollecting everything there is to remember about a person, place or thing, or an event.

Take a piece of paper and write your topic in the center. Draw a circle (balloon) around it.

Then sit quietly for a few moments with your eyes closed, taking deep breaths and exhaling slowly, feeling your body become more relaxed with each breath.

Start thinking about the topic you've selected. The memories will come in a flood.

Open your eyes and grab a pen. As soon as a thought comes to you, jot it down, somewhere on the paper. Don't worry about where. Don't censor yourself, even if the thought seems silly or way off base, or you'll stop the flow.

As you're writing one thing, three others will pop into your head, so just keep writing as fast as you can. Use abbreviations, shorthand or one-word memory joggers.

When you've exhausted all your memories of that topic, draw a balloon around each one. Look over the balloons and notice which ones are related. You can cluster them in your mind, draw strings attaching them, or color code them. (Some will overlap.)

You'll find that you have an abundance of memories and details to draw from. You don't have to use all, or any, of the things you wrote down, but you've got them if you want them.

To illustrate the Balloon Method, I have done the exercise using my childhood bedroom, which I shared with my sister, as my topic.

For this book I didn't abbreviate or use shorthand as much as I normally would.

After completing this exercise I have plenty to think about. Now I can select from these many aspects of my room to flesh out stories of my childhood/teenage years. (I used some of these recollections in *Miss Rogers Stinks.*)

The "balloon" items were very useful in creating a vivid impression of that room. I hope my readers experience it along with me.

FRINGE BENEFITS

My greatest reward as the teacher of memoir-writing classes is to watch my students' growth in competence and confidence. Many of them come nervously to the first class, lacking conviction that their life's experiences are worthy of recording and anxious about their ability to write them.

Through the process of writing their stories and sharing them with their classmates, they come to recognize and acknowledge that they are indeed special, unique individuals, and that others really are interested in what they have to say. They become convinced that they can tell their own and their family's stories better than anyone else, and gain the self-assurance to do it.

In the process, they learn that writing is no big deal -- nothing to get uptight about. They learn that writing and sharing their stories is a lot of fun.

As their classmates validate their life-experiences an unexpected fringe benefit becomes apparent. Their self-esteem and sense of self-worth begin to blossom. As they share their stories with their families, whose responses are also positive, their self-regard and self-respect are further enhanced. Their children and grandchildren, their friends and neighbors, are impressed with the wonderful, sometimes amazing things they are learning about them. All this makes them feel quite proud and pleased with themselves.

This unanticipated outcome is the greatest payoff for me, and for them, as well. So, please be aware that you are not just writing your life stories for other people, even if that was your original objective. You are doing it for yourself as well. What a great way to spend your "prime-time" years, engaging in an activity that makes you feel good about yourself and your life.

In addition, writing one's autobiography is tremendously helpful in keeping the brain and memory functioning. You'll find that as you employ conscious recall you will spontaneously remember incidents and people you hadn't thought of in 30, 40, 50 years, or more. One memory leads to another. You'll recall friends and all sorts of things you thought you'd forgotten, and more than likely, you're going to enjoy the heck out of it.

As you're writing about your life, chances are excellent that you will learn a great deal about yourself. The more you write the more you'll learn. You'll find that patterns will emerge and you'll get some "Aha!s" -- revelations about yourself, your relationships, and your life.

In addition, writing greatly increases one's powers of observation and communication. You'll find yourself watching and listening closely to whatever's happening around you so that you'll be able to describe things more clearly and completely.

Furthermore, writing one's life experience, especially a not-so-pleasant memory, is cathartic. It's as if, by getting it down on paper or onto a computer chip, you're getting it out of your system -- out of your psyche -- and letting it go. Many a writer has reported this, and I've experienced it myself.

In writing about an old trauma or an old enemy, you finally release it, eliminating its power over you. You may find, some time after writing it, that the emotional charge is gone. Finally, it is just another of life's many experiences. Your grief, anger, or torment is greatly diminished if not eliminated.

An article in the (April 1999) Journal of the American Medical Association (JAMA) tells of an experiment in which patients with one of two chronic conditions -- rheumatoid arthritis or asthma

-- were asked to write. Half wrote about a "stressful" event, the other half about something neutral, for twenty minutes, three days in a row. They were then tested periodically over the next four months. The group writing about a trauma showed dramatic reduction in their symptoms. The other group did not.

In my opinion, nearly any illness can be helped by conducting a similar program. Those experimenters focused on just two of the many chronic illnesses from which people suffer. I bet the results would be the same for other chronic illnesses, too. Why not give it a try? You have nothing to lose, except maybe pain and suffering.

Even if the stories of your traumas and tragedies don't make the final cut and are never seen in your finished work, the emotional result is the same. It's good therapy.

Writing is a form of therapy; sometimes I wonder how all those people who do not write, compose or paint can manage to escape the madness, the melancholia, the panic-fear which is inherent in a human situation.

Graham Greene

Writing Activity #4

• Write a story about "your war."

In this book are two stories about the authors' World War II experiences, "I'll Never Drive in L.A." by Leta Wright, and "Crossing the Rhine " by Jackson Clarke, and another which took place during the Korean Conflict: "The Best Meal I Ever Had," by Lawrence Green. Their stories and their writing styles differ greatly, but all are excellent personal histories which add to our knowledge of those eras.

Whatever your war was called, write about your war experience: something that occurred, something you did, something someone else did, the mood in the country.

On the following page are some of my recollections of WWII. I was just a kid, living in the USA, so my participation was at a distance. But it's part of my history, and it may add to the overall picture of that era.

Write a piece -- a story, an anecdote, a series of recollections -- based on your war experience.

Have fun!

YOU'RE THE STAR!

The subject of your memoirs is, of course, you. You are the central character, the protagonist, the star!

You are the center of the universe. All the other characters revolve around you as the planets revolve around the sun.

All the events of your lifetime exist in relation to you: where you were and what you were doing when they happened; how you felt about and responded to them; how they influenced or affected you; the conflicts or struggles they caused.

When you begin to see your own life as grist for the literary mill, everything changes. You begin to perceive just about everything as a possible story.

If you're like most people, as you start shining the spotlight on the events and experiences of your life, you'll begin to realize just how fascinating you and your life really are.

SEDUCE YOUR READERS

How do you go about writing a memoir people will want to read? You reach into your bag of tricks (provided throughout this book) and pull them out, one by one, time and again. First and foremost is the fine art of seduction.

Surely you know how to be seductive. You simply promise more than you're willing to deliver at the moment. A woman may coquettishly drop a strap from her shoulder while delivering a smouldering look, then demurely pull it back up . . . with an unspoken promise in her eyes.

By now she's got the attention of the object of her seduction. He's positively panting to find out what she will deliver . . . and when. If she's smart, she'll keep him guessing for a while.

What works in the romantic arena works in the literary one as well. You tease the reader. You make promises for later fulfillment. You drop little hints of things to come.

You allude to the things you'll surrender later -- just enough to lead your reader on -- then sidestep the issue, for now, moving onto something else. In other words, you play hard to get.

You tease, entice, tantalize. You lead your readers down the primrose path. You do what is necessary to keep them wanting more.

In your relationship with your readers, as in any relationship, you don't want to give away too much too soon. The reader will lose interest if you're "too easy" -- if you give everything away up front.

So go ahead, seduce your readers. Make promises, promises . . . holding back, keeping something in reserve.

But please, before it's over, make good on your promises.

SPICE UP YOUR LIFE!

Here's the bag of tricks I promised; strategies for spicing up your stories and keeping your readers turning those pages.

There's always more than one way to say anything. You can write a story in such a way that it is bland as milk toast, or you can turn it into a tangy jambalaya. As you're writing your stories and painting the scenes of your life with sufficient detail so that your reader experiences them along with you, here are some tricks you can pull out of your bag to spice 'em up.

Incongruities & Paradoxes - Mystery & Intrigue

From time to time, draw readers in with a bit of mystery -- a touch of intrigue. Write your introduction to a section, chapter or vignette in such a way that there are incongruities designed to pique the readers' curiosity, causing them to ask, "What is wrong with this picture?" making them wonder "Why is this person (or thing) out of place, out of sync? What's going on here?" This is bound to keep your readers flipping pages in order to solve the mystery. The following is such a paradox:

A Bizarre Ritual

Despite the warmth of the summer evening, an icy shiver went through me as I crouched behind the ancient tombstone, making myself as small as I could. A ghostly moan hung over the graveyard; goose pimples popped out on my bare arms. I gave no thought to my formal gown or the gardenia pinned to it.

Pressing against the rough granite marker, I held my breath. The earth vibrated with heavy footfalls as the boy came nearer ... nearer ... ever nearer.

* * *

The writer (me) hopes the reader will wonder why this girl, dressed in a formal gown, is hiding in a graveyard at night: who is after her, and why.

I hope the reader will be sufficiently intrigued to keep reading so as to learn the answers too those questions.

In case you are, here's the rest of the story:

He was so close I could have reached out and touched him, but he didn't see me. He went on past. At last, I started to breathe again.

A voice called from the portico of the mausoleum, directly across West Belmont. "Carol, you're next." My heart thumping, my hands cold and clammy, I stood up on trembling legs, smoothed my skirt, and left my hiding place, secure in the knowledge that the call gave me immunity from my stalker.

But across the road at the mausoleum a far greater terror lay in store. I wanted to turn tail and run but didn't dare. I hurried past the headstones, stumbling over the uneven burial plots in the old cemetery. The filmy material of my full skirt caught on something. I gave it a yank and ran on, unwilling to make them wait. That would only make it worse.

Pulling open the heavy doors to the great room, I tiptoed in and sank onto a chair at the rear. Up front were two black-lacquered grand pianos where the casket ought to be, their lids up-tilted, flanked by sprays of violet gladiolas left from someone's funeral, no doubt. A blond girl about my age, in yellow organdy and black patent Mary Janes, sat at one of the pianos, playing her recital piece. She lost her place and had to start over, a chilling reminder of my own worst nightmare.

I tried to calm myself as I waited my turn, taking deep breaths and exhaling slowly, my hands pressed against my thighs to quell their quivering. The girl finished and with a Thank God it's over! expression, stood and curtsied as we girls had been taught, and bolted for the door.

The person responsible for this bizarre ritual, Bessie Anderson, my piano teacher, stood elegant and formidable in long black crepe, reading from the program. She announced, "Carol Petersen will play 'Barcarolle,' by Jacques Offenbach."

Making my way up the center aisle with all the enthusiasm of the condemned approaching the guillotine, I reached the piano and sat down. Positioning my trembling fingers over the keys while my foot stretched for the pedal, I started to play the piece I'd practiced and practiced.

Mrs. Anderson, organist for most of Fresno's funerals, could hold her annual recital in the funeral parlor of her choice. She always chose this Spanish Mission-style mausoleum, which her young students were dying to explore. Off the foyer, to the right, were thick glass doors through which a long marble corridor was visible. Inside the walls were crypts (boxes) filled with dead people. Then, to the left, through another thick glass door, down another long corridor, was the crematorium where, we were told, huge ovens turned dead bodies into "gritty little piles of ashes."

The adolescents among us regaled us younger kids with visions of ghosts and ghouls, and chanted,

"The worms crawl in, the worms crawl out,

The worms play tiddlywinks on your snout . . ."

Right across the road was Mountain View Cemetery where, between our musical tortures, we played "Hide and Go Seek" among the tombstones. It was great spooky fun.

* * *

So you see, once in a while, it's fun to play with a story and tell it in such a way as to hook the readers like big fish, then reel 'em in. I could have told the story "straight," and it would been no more, no less true. But it wouldn't have been as much fun for either the writer or the reader.

Similes, Analogies & Metaphors

The use of simile, analogy or metaphor can make a passage more descriptive and visual. All three are devices through which writers give their readers images to relate to, presenting a clear and colorful mental picture. They are ways of using similarities, comparisons or representations to spice up your writing. It's not necessary to know which is which, but only to be aware of them as techniques to make your stories more interesting and fun to read.

The following over-simplifications give you the idea:

Similes

A simile compares one thing to another using as:

• Dad came home drunk *as* a sailor on shore leave.

• She was as mean *as* a cornered alley cat.

Analogies

An analogy is something that is *like* something else:

• Her smile was *like* a halogen lamp in a coal mine.

• That pile of straw felt *like* a feather bed that night.

Metaphors

A metaphor compares a thing to an unrelated concept with shared characteristics, as if it *were* that thing, e.g:

• A mighty fortress *is* our God.

• Her lips *were* ripe, luscious plums.

• The sky *is* an upside-down bowl.

In each case, the writer conveys the message that the subject has the qualities of the metaphor, e.g; Our god is a mighty fortress, i.e., strong, protective, enduring.

Her lips make you think of ripe, luscious plums, therefore, metaphorically, they are ripe, luscious plums.

Throw 'em a Curve

Every once in awhile, do the unexpected. Throw in an image that will catch your reader off guard. Be a little unpredictable. The trick is to come up with an image that's out of whack, that pulls readers up short and makes them think. E.g:

• "Jane is as easy as the TV Guide's Crossword Puzzle."

• "'Oh Trevor, take me,' she panted, her bosom heaving like a college freshman on Dollar-a-Beer Night."

(Those came in an email. I don't know the author, but I couldn't resist using them.)

Surprise your readers. Startle them a little. As in the above sentences, *double entendre** delivers a curve ball. When you throw one at your readers it wakes them up, puts smiles on their faces, and has them wanting more.

* Double entendre: a word or phrase with double meanings, e.g: easy and heaving. The writer exploited double entendre for maximum impact.

Modifiers

Modifiers are descriptive words or phrases used to define, explain or illustrate what you're talking about. They are another way of spicing up your story. With modifiers you can convey a great deal of information and make your story ever-so-much more interesting.

Take this basic sentence: *When I got home from my date my mother met me on the porch,* and modify it. Here are three examples (modifiers in italics):

- When I got home from my *very first date*, my mother met Sid and me on the *wisteria-draped front* porch with a *warm* smile and *cold* root beer floats.

- When I got home from my date at 3:00 a.m., *a bit* tipsy, my mother, in her *dopey* pin curls and *ratty old* bathrobe, met me on the porch, raving *like a lunatic*.

- When I got home from my *clandestine* date, my *hysterical* mother met me on the *dark* porch, both furious and relieved.

Each of these sentences portrays a very different scenario and produces a very different feeling. The basic sentence is the same. The only difference is the modifiers. Their use sets the mood and describes the setting, the people and their emotions, efficiently relating a huge amount of information, all of which makes for a stronger, more interesting story.

So, rather than just stating the basic facts, spice them up and flesh them out with descriptive, explanatory and illustrative words and phrases.

Note: Limit your use of adverbs and adjectives to what's necessary to set the scene. Overuse of them is the mark of an amateur.

Synonyms

Synonyms are words or phrases that mean the same, or nearly the same, thing. For example, fate and destiny are synonyms; mystified and bewildered are synonyms. Their use keeps you from being repetitive and dull. But even more important, it allows you to shade the meaning or mood of a passage and/or make it more specific, thereby making your writing more engaging.

In the second modified sentence on the previous page, the word "tipsy" is used to indicate a level of intoxication. You might try substituting others which do the same thing to see how they change the meaning or the mood of the sentence or reveal the writer's intention, e.g., drunk, soused, bleary-eyed, snockered, falling-down, pie-eyed, boozed-up.

One can imagine that a synonym such as "snockered" might have been more accurate, but the writer was attempting to portray herself in a good light, so "tipsy" was the word she chose.

Each word choice may alter the feeling or impression of a sentence ever so slightly, yet ever so importantly.

In the next section you'll learn where to find all the synonyms you'll ever need or want.

Cliffhangers

One surefire way to keep your readers turning pages is to end a section in a cliffhanger.

When I was a kid there were Saturday afternoon serials at the movie theaters in which every episode ended with the hero in dire straits, sometimes literally hanging off a cliff by his or her fingernails, with the villain about to stomp on them.

Just as we couldn't wait to get back to the movie theater the following week, so will your readers be eager to find out what happens next.

In other words, don't wrap everything up too neatly or too quickly. Build tension, create suspense, anticipation. Make your readers sweat, wondering what the outcome will be. End your chapter or section at a crucial moment.

Dialogue

Dialogue (conversation) adds spice to your literary soup, so don't hesitate to put words in your characters' mouths.

Now, I realize you may not remember exactly what someone said fifty years ago, or even what was said over this morning's Raisin-Bran. But you remember the gist of the conversation -- enough to fill in the gaps. All writers exercise "literary license" to jazz up their stories.

When you write what someone said, your stories are far more involving than if you just write *about* what someone says. Which of the following two sentences is more interesting?

My father indicated that I should either get a job or find another place to live.

Or this one:

Dad said, "Get a job or get out."

I think you'll agree that while the second example delivers the same message as the first, it does so with more pizazz. You actually get a mental picture of "Dad" saying it.

Dialogue is also useful in bringing out someone's personality and character. For example:

Grandpa said, "I always said Jake was gonna live forever, 'cause he's too dang mean to die."

Or:

Grandpa declared, "The world is a far better place because of Jake. With his passing it is much improved."

Here we have two Grandpas expressing the same feeling about Jake. Their speech reveals a great deal about them. The first appears to be a cantankerous old guy who "tells it like it is," while the second seems somewhat philosophical and subtly humorous. That was accomplished merely through dialogue -- by putting words in their mouths.

The writer could have just said, "Grandpa didn't like Jake." But dialogue allows "Grandpa" to develop into a real person.

Dialogue is one of the most useful tools a writer has for spicing up a story and bringing the characters to life. Use it.

Writing Activity #5

Write a story in which you use Paradox or Inconsistency to hook your reader in.

The topic can be anything. If you need help with a story idea, look through the list in "What to Write About", or the section on "Where to Get Ideas."

• Plant doubt or confusion in your readers' minds. Make them ask, "What is wrong with this picture?"

• Play a trick on your readers. Make them think you're talking about one thing when you're actually talking about something else. But please clear up the confusion before the conclusion.

• Use as many of the other "Spice Up Your Life" techniques as you can.

• Have fun!

ALL THOSE FANCY WORDS

I often hear, "I can't write. I don't know all those fancy words."

Relax. You don't need to. Some of the most endearing and enduring literature is written with common, ordinary, garden-variety words.

Take *The Adventures of Tom Sawyer,* by Mark Twain. Are there any words in it you couldn't, or wouldn't, have written? (Well, maybe a few, but that's because it was written in the 19th century and uses words we now consider "quaint."

Part of the reason it is so well-loved and wears so well is that it is simply written. It doesn't try to impress anyone with a lot of four-bit words. It tells the story of a 10-year-old boy who lived in a small midwestern town in the mid-19th century. Although Samuel Clemens (Mark Twain) had a "fancy" vocabulary, he chose to tell this story plainly. And because it is the story of plain folks in a plain town, telling it that way makes it all the more powerful.

As a writer, however, you want to keep your story interesting, so you won't want to use the same word over and over and over (except where you need to for emphasis or to make a point, as I just did).

The best writers' aid I've found is *The Synonym Finder* (J.I. Rodale, Rodale Press, Emmaus, PA, 1978.) You just look up the word you're thinking of and it provides more synonyms than you'll ever need.

For example, you may need a synonym for tension. I chose it because it is one of the shorter selections.

tension, *n. 1. tautness, tightness, extension, distension, elongation; pull, tug, yank, strain; stretch, draw, traction, tensity.*
2. anxiety, uneasiness, disquiet, disquietude, inquietude, fretfulness; worry, trouble, concern, vexation, pressure, stress, heat, burden, cross, encumbrance, cumbrance, nervousness, ants. Inf. butterflies. Sl. habdabs; excitement, agitation, perturbation, suspense, anticipation, expectation, apprehension, fear.

(Note: Computers have made it easy to find synonyms. Just type the word in the search engine (Google, Yahoo, etc.), with "synonym," (e.g: "tension -- synonym)," and you'll have instant access. However, Rodale's *Synonym Finder* is by far the best resource, in my opinion.

As you write you'll probably notice that your vocabulary increases. You may even discover that words can be fun. You may start making a mental note or jotting down a word or phrase when you hear one that is especially powerful, descriptive, or appropriate.

ORGANIZING YOUR LIFE STORIES

Chronological Order

There are many ways to organize an autobiography or memoir. There is, of course, the old standard, tried and true Chronological order, starting at your birth (or an earlier time, if you're including your family's history), and moving through time.

There's a lot to be said for this order of things. It provides a structural framework on which to build your story and can be combined with any number of styles and forms.

It is not without peril, though. The danger is that you may be tempted to simply note the events of your life chronologically, e.g: I was born in Poughkeepsie in 1950; I started Kindergarten in 1955; in 1962 I got a two-wheel bike; I moved to Detroit in 1966 and got my first Ford; in 1968 I left high school and joined the Navy; I served in Viet Nam; I enrolled at Michigan State in 1971.

Never, *never*, *never* do that. That's a laundry list -- and it's a real yawner. It tells nothing about you, nor does it make the reader want to know about you -- even those who love you. I suppose it's better than nothing, but not much. What it tells the reader is, this person is a colossal bore. Now, you and I both know you're not, but you sure couldn't tell it from that.

There are many things you can do to avoid the "laundry list" approach to autobiography. For one thing, instead of saying, "I was born on . . ." tell a story about it, e.g:

"The night before I was born the Great Blizzard of '59 came through. Early next morning, Dad and Granddad shoveled snow, 6' deep, all the way to the main road, about 100 yards, so Doc Hammill could get up to 28 Gooseberry Lane and give Mom a hand."

Or:

"My parents hadn't even thought about boys' names. They knew I was going to be a girl. They kept blaming each other for having another boy and fighting about it. So after two weeks I was still nameless. Grandma lost patience with them and made out the birth certificate herself. She named me for her movie idol, Rudolf Valentino."

As you've seen, throughout this book are ways to show your reader how interesting you and your life are -- devices through which to breathe life into your stories, to transport your readers into a scene, to elicit their emotions, to make them want to know more about you. Read on.

By Theme

What's your passion? What is there that has been a constant throughout most of your life? You may decide to write your stories according to a theme, choosing a thread that runs through your life and using it to tie your stories together. For instance:

• Career: You may want to make your career a major character in your story, telling how it has taken you through life or, if you've changed careers, how your career choices came about and how they have impacted your life. You may want to draw a parallel between your personal growth and your career path.

• Animals: Perhaps you're an animal lover. You story would be incomplete without the animals that have been part of your life.

• Adventure: Are you an adventurer? Your life story will certainly be about your grand adventures, because that's who you are. Your adventures tell their own tale.

• Parties, Social Events: If you're the host or hostess with the mostest, you may want to tell your life story by relating the great parties you've thrown, including guest lists, food served, decorations, etc. You'll definitely want to talk about the function of an event -- its purpose or reason for being, and include anecdotes from it.

• Clothes: Do you adore clothes? Your theme could involve the outfit or ensemble you were wearing for the important events of your life, perhaps with photos or sketches.

• Cars: Are cars your passion? You may relate the events of your life to the car you were driving when they occurred. Or you may tell about the acquisition and restoration of your cars, or your adventures with them.

• Airplanes: Did you experience "love at first flight?" (Or the opposite? Do you experience "fear of flying?") If so, write about the planes and flights of your life, where they took you, your flying exploits.

• Films: If you're a movie buff you could relate your life's events to the movies and movie stars of your life, including insights on how they influenced you.

• Sports: Is sports in general, or a specific sport, your passion? That may be the thread that runs through your life stories.

• ~~Dis~~ability: Did/do you have what society deems a "disability?" Your readers will want to know about the challenges you've faced and how you've dealt with them. They'll want to know how your "disability" has affected your life, how it has (or has not) defined you, as well as your reflections on it.

• Minority: Are you a member of a racial, ethnic, religious, gender or sexual-orientation group toward which society's attitude and/or laws have discriminated? Your theme could well be the societal changes (or lack thereof) and relevant turning points you have witnessed or participated in, or the discrimination you've experienced, what it's done to you, and what/how you've felt and done about it. Tell your story.

• Collectibles: If you're a collector, talk about your collection(s). As you write about each piece, you'll be telling about yourself; about your stage in life, where you were and what you were doing, what you were thinking and feeling as each item became part of your collection.

• Music: Music is an enormous part of life for many of us. You can write your story in terms of the music that touched you at each step.

Play with the idea. The bottom line is, it's your life and your life story. Make it truly yours by telling about the things that matter to you. Let your readers in on who you are and what you care about. Give them indications of what it (your theme) has meant to you and how it affected your life. It will give them insights into the real you.

You'll see, as you're writing, that just about any theme will work. And as you write about your theme you can place it in the personal and worldwide events of your lifetime.

Comparative

One of the benefits of having lived a long time is that of acquiring a unique perspective or frame of reference. You've lived in the most amazing period in all of history. The last 100 years have seen the first manned flight, the first transoceanic flight, the first jet airplane, the first spaceships, men walking on the moon, spaceships landing on Mars and photographing Venus.

A short 100 years ago, very few households had electricity or indoor plumbing, a telephone or an automobile. Many of the things we now take for granted were then the stuff of science fiction. Now that we are in the 21st century, the majority of homes in America has at least one computer with instantaneous worldwide internet access, a stereophonic or multi-phonic sound system, electronic games and cellular phones.

We have gone from "a glimpse of stocking" as shocking to "anything goes." We now accept full nudity and steamy sex scenes in movies and even on TV sitcoms. We've gone from a time when a relatively mild profanity -- "Frankly, my dear, I don't give a damn." -- nearly blocked the release of a spectacular film, to the point, now, where every second word in some movies is .

. . well, you know. It's no longer considered shocking. "Anything goes" is a fact of modern life.

Much less than 100 years ago in the U.S., social, political, economic and legal discrimination against non-males, non-Christians, non-heterosexuals, and persons of non-European descent was the norm, sanctioned by law and accepted by society. Now, while it hasn't totally disappeared, such discrimination is at least generally illegal. Our "collective consciousness" has raised to the point where it's no longer acceptable to the majority.

Having lived through this, we have achieved a perspective which enables us to discuss our earlier actions, attitudes and customs, on both a personal and societal level, and report on the changes. We're able to compare our former selves with our present selves, previous times with the present, prior biases and prejudices with current attitudes, former mores with current ones, and tell how those changes have affected our lives.

Personal Essays

If writing your memoirs, per se, doesn't appeal to you, there are other options, such as personal essays -- "think pieces" -- your opinions about anything and everything.

The great 19th century American essayist, Ralph Waldo Emerson, never wrote an autobiography, yet we know a great deal about him through his essays. He left a rich and varied legacy that gives readers tremendous insight into the era in which he lived, what he thought about a great many things, how he felt about the issues of the day, as well as his viewpoint on the great philosophical quandaries of the ages.

Do you remember Erma Bombeck? (A columnist in the '50s - '70s) We felt as if we knew her, almost as if she were a member of our family or a dear coffee-klatch neighbor. Personal essays were her forte. She just wrote about common, ordinary, everyday things: kids, husband, PTA meetings, the family cat, the family dog, the family septic tank -- things we could relate to. A great many of us felt so close to her that we mourned her death. That was because she had shared herself with us through her essays.

So, rather than get involved in writing the stories of your life, you may wish to write your thoughts, feelings and emotions about all kinds of things. Pretend you're a newspaper or magazine columnist: pick a topic a week and explore it in writing.

This could be your legacy, and what a wonderful legacy it will be.

The Combination Plate

The combination of any or all of the above ways of creating your legacy is perfectly acceptable. If you are writing your memoirs you may wish to include an occasional "think piece" among your life stories and recollections. It will help round out the picture of you for your readers.

Remember, this is your creation and it can be as unique as you are.

Writing Activity #6

Write a story in which a vehicle (car, truck, plane, train, boat, bicycle*) played a part.

Be sure to tell (if appropriate):
- How/when it came into your life.
- What it looked like: and the make, model, year.
- What was unique or unusual about it.
- How you felt when you were in/on it.
- An adventure related to it.
- Any trouble or conflict it caused you.

On upcoming pages are two examples of stories involving a vehicle. One is from the male point of view, the other female -- altogether different, as you'll notice.

* One of my students wrote her vehicle story about her trip from the entrance of the ER to the Operating Room on a hospital gurney.
* Another wrote about his roller skates.

HOW DO YOU EAT AN ELEPHANT?

Do you feel overwhelmed by the fact that there's so much to write about, or that there are so many options for writing it? How on earth are you supposed to write about your life?

It's like the old riddle, How do you eat an elephant? The answer: *One bite at a time.* Just write:

- One sentence at a time.
- One scene at a time.
- One event at a time.
- One unforgettable character at a time.

The bag of tricks I gave you earlier to spice up your memoirs will make them more interesting and exciting. But right now, I'm urging you to just get started. Just start writing. Just get your recollections on paper or computer. You can go back later and spice them up. You can fill in the gaps and details later. And you can edit and tighten up your work when you're nearly done.

It's probably important that you rewrite it, but to get started, just get started.

Just start writing.

Rewriting

It's said that great novels are not written; they are rewritten. The same is true of good memoirs. You will no doubt want, at some point, to make corrections, additions and deletions. Ultimately, you will have a really good finished product. But don't feel that you must write it in its finished form the first time through. All writers rewrite and revise.

> *I have written, often several times,*
> *every word I have ever published.*
> *My pencils outlast their erasers.*
> Vladimir Nobokov

To get started you must get something in writing. You can't change something that doesn't exist. As long as it's just an idea floating around in your head, no matter how profound it may be, there's nothing of substance to work with. So get your idea, your basic story, down on paper. Then go back and change it, adding wonderful details and descriptions, all of which will help make it *really good.*

As you do so you still see it growing into something you'll be proud of. And you will see yourself growing into a writer, a real writer, with your own style and flair.

Unless you have a publishing house making the decisions on your work, you are the one who decides when a story, chapter or segment is done. You may do as little or as much rewriting as you feel comfortable with. (Unless you have an editor, which I recommend.)

As you're writing, editing and rewriting, all the while developing your own style, you'll appreciate all the help you can get. The beauty of modern computer technology is that you needn't feel that whatever you write is carved in Mt. Rushmore. It's simple to change whatever you have written. You can make corrections, move paragraphs or chapters willy-nilly, take the beginning and put it at the end, and insert or delete a word, sentence or chapter whenever and wherever you want to.

I recommend becoming computer-literate for this project if you haven't already done so. Many extremely mature adults have and it has changed and enriched their lives. Along with a computer for researching and doing the actual writing of it, a scanner and color printer will enable you to include photographs and other memorabilia, which will enhance your finished edition.

However, as you know, people have been writing without benefit of computers, scanners and color printers for centuries and have created great works. So don't let the fact that you have no computer or computer skills stop you. While a computer makes it easier, it's not essential. It matters not whether you write on a yellow legal pad, a typewriter, or the newest, zingiest computer.

In short, don't place obstacles in your way. Just get started;

just do it.

One bite at a time.

BE NATURAL

You can be a little ungrammatical if you
come from the right part of the country.
Robert Frost

Don't be afraid to be your own natural self. You want your readers to know who you are, so don't leave out the colorful speech patterns, the colloquialisms and dialect, the quaint or quirky expressions used in your part of the country or by you and your family, words and phrases used in your era.

The following is an example of writing naturally, from Freddie Mae Baxter's autobiography, *The Seventh Child: A Lucky Life*.

When I was growing up you better not say anything about sex. You didn't ask no questions then. You didn't ask, "Momma, how to you get to be momma?" or "Momma, where do babies come from?" . . . In those days, when we started getting a little sassy around the pants, they'd say, "Keep your dress down . . ." but they didn't want to tell you why we should keep our dress down. You couldn't ask.

~~~~~

Notice how you get a real feel for this person because she

writes as she speaks. And the phrase "a little sassy around the pants" is so expressive I can't help visualizing that sassy little girl swaying her little hips and swishing her little skirt in that flirty way little girls do.

With that charming colloquialism, Freddie Mae Baxter creates a picture in her reader's mind worth a whole lot of words.

A man who writes well writes not as others write,
but as he himself writes.
It is often in speaking badly that he speaks well.

Montesquieu

Your memoir is an extension of you. Through it people will get to know you, so write as you speak.

Ernest Hemingway said this of his writing style:

In stating as fully as I could how things really were it was very difficult and I wrote awkwardly and the awkwardness is that they called my style. All mistakes and awkwardness are easy to see, and they called it "style."

The following is an excerpt from Will James' book, *Lone Cowboy*. It is a fine example of writing naturally.

One day in our ramblings through that country we run acrost a whole town, the first town I'd ever seen, and it was deserted . . .

but I got a big thrill looking through it. I'd never seen such big houses as was there, two and three floors high, and whole rows of 'em with no space between. . . . Some was made out of brick and stone, with big high steel shutters on the windows, and steel doors. I wondered what was inside of them.

In the houses I could get into I found enough things new and of interest to keep me exploring forever, I thought. There was fancy chairs and bedsteads, bureaus and dressers with some clothes still in 'em, pictures on the wall, and everything that's in any home where folks live steady, from the top story down to the cellar.

In some places there was pianos and pump organs. Bopy made me acquainted with them music boxes and for awhile I had a lot of fun making noise. But I never was cut out to handle music, so after awhile, I went on exploring some more. I was looking for the big houses now, with the fancy front porch, because them always had good pictures on the walls inside, and the part of town where the shacks was didn't interest me no more.

Writing Activity #7

Write about an object, an item, a thing.

Pick something you'd like to write about, something you own, once owned, or aspired to own, or something your family owned: a piece of furniture, jewelry, china, silver, art, clothing, a toy, car, boat or plane, a collectible, a house or piece of property -- anything.

Write about (for example):

• What you know of its history.

• What is unique or special about it.

• How/When it came into your/your family's possession, if it did.

• What it means or meant to you/your family and why.

• Special occasions you associate with it, if any.

• The people you associate with it, if any.

• Have fun!

THE QUESTIONS YOU MUST ANSWER

Who, What, When, Where & Why are known as "The Five 'W's' of Writing." They are the questions which must be answered in every story. This is the first lesson in Journalism 101. These questions must be addressed or there's no story. The reader needs to know:

- *Who* the story is about. In most cases, in your memoir, it is you. But there are probably other people in your stories too. You need to let the reader know just who you are and who those other people are.
- What the story is about -- its subject matter.
- Where your story takes place -- its setting.
- When your story takes place -- its time frame.
- Why you wrote the story -- its point. (Also, why your characters do what they do.)

I'm going to add a sixth "W of Writing" -- How. (Hold it up to a mirror.)

How the story unfolds -- how goals are accomplished, how things get done, how the hero's transformation occurs.

We'll discuss these more later.

CONTEXT

Context is simply the time and place -- the when and where -- of your story. Placing your life's adventures in context gives them added authenticity and credibility.

It's a good idea to weave the events of the day into your stories: the songs, movies, Broadway shows, cars, toys, radio or TV shows, styles and fashions, fads, hairstyles, appliances, celebrities and politicians, as well as landmarks to identify the places in which the story occurs.

Some of it you may remember, like where you were when you learned that the Twin Towers were attacked, or what song was popular the week of your senior prom. Those are the easy things. There are plenty of other things you'll want to include, details that will make your story more engaging and help people relate to it, but most of us need a little help remembering them.

A little research will help refresh your memory. Of course, the internet is the easiest, quickest way to research nearly anything. You can simply Google, Bing, or Yahoo it. But you may need or want to do further digging at:

- *Old catalogs*, such as Sears & Roebuck, will provide all manner of references for your stories. Some of those old catalogs have been reissued in commemorative editions.

- Your *local library*. More than likely, your library has copies of old newspapers, catalogs and magazines, dating all the way back to Day-One, stored on microfiche.

- Your town's *historical society* is a great resource. It can supply the details that lend authority and local tid-bits to your life stories. If you no longer live in the town you're writing about, it's still your best bet. If possible, go there and pay a visit to the historical society. And while you're there, try to establish a relationship with someone who works there. Then, when you leave, you'll have a friendly, helpful connection with whom you can stay in touch by phone or email to get your questions answered. They'll also provide old photos of your town, and maybe even your relatives.

The following is an excerpt from one of my mini-memoirs, demonstrating the use of context:

It was 1956, late November, hardly the best time to cross the north Atlantic. John and I had traveled by train from Darmstadt to Bremerhaven (Germany), then transferred onto an army ship.

An army ship?! It was obvious that this was not a Navy ship or an ocean liner since it was anything but "ship shape." It was butt-ugly; it was dirty; and it was slow.

Since John was a lowly enlisted man we were separated during the long voyage home. He bunked with hundreds of other enlisted men down in the ship's hold while I shared a "stateroom" with other enlisted men's dependents. It had two sets of metal Army bunk-beds under which we stored our suitcases.

Even in the best of circumstances, an ocean voyage can be boring. And this was hardly the best of circumstances.

One day another ship passed us, which caused great excitement. Everyone rushed out on deck. We waved and hollered to the passengers of the other vessel who waved and hollered back; the ships whistled and tooted at one another. The only problem was that the ship passing us was going the same direction we were -- sailing from Europe to the east coast of the U.S. It glided past as if we were standing still.

We had left Germany just after the Hungarian uprising and were concerned we'd be held up by it. Our government had promised to help Hungary's freedom fighters if they would revolt against the communists. All the men aboard this vessel had been poised to go to Hungary to fight if the US government had kept its promise. But it hadn't. So we were going home, but fully expected the ship to turn around should the powers-that-be change their minds.

Cut off from the world, we were hungry for news. Just before our departure President Dwight Eisenhower and Vice-President Richard Nixon had been reelected. . . . Elvis Presley was hotter than hot; any news of him was titillating. Movie Star Grace Kelly and Prince Rainier of Monaco were newlyweds and we gals were eager for news of this fairytale couple.

A few days out there was a "news bulletin" -- news more

startling than anything we'd imagined. Through word of mouth we learned that Elvis Presley was dead. Word of it spread with the speed of light, sending shock waves through the ship. No details were offered, so there was a great deal of speculation as to the how, why, when and where of it. The ship buzzed with it.

We rolled on, one storm after another, one Parchesi game after another, one shivering walk around the deck after another, one boring day after another. Interspersed with all this were our reminiscences of Elvis, including his songs: Heartbreak Hotel, You Ain't Nuthin But a Hound Dog, Love Me Tender Love me Sweet, and Don't You Step on my Blue Suede Shoes. A lot of head-shaking accompanied any discussion of him. We couldn't believe it.

Finally, the long voyage neared its end. We hauled our bags out on deck. A tugboat escorted us into the New York harbor where the Statue of Liberty welcomed us home. By that time we were celebrating getting off that damn boat as much as getting back to "the land of round doorknobs" -- the good old U.S.A.

We were soon to rejoin the world and learn what had happened since we had, for all intents and purposes, left it a full two weeks earlier. Now, whoever had circulated the story of Elvis' untimely death saw fit to reveal the rest of the story.

'Elvis had a heart attack' (pause for effect) 'when his hound dog shit on his blue suede shoes.'

Oh no! We'd been duped. This was indeed a ship of fools. But we had a good laugh out of it.

You can see how, by mentioning current events, songs and celebrities of the day, along with the cities, a well-known land-mark, and the vast ocean to indicate location, the story's context is set. The reader gets a feeling for its time and place.

LIFE PATTERNS

One of the many advantages of living a long life is that we can notice patterns -- repetitive behaviors -- and begin to make some sense out of them. From the vantage point of your present self you may be able to look back and discern one or more of the patterns in your life. One of them may provide the jumping off point for your memoir and its framework. Discussing a life pattern will allow you to become a bit introspective, which is not a bad thing in autobiographic writing.

The following discussion of one of my patterns is the Preface for my memoirs:

My mother used to say, "Carol can do anything she wants to. She just doesn't want to do very much." Little did she know.

The truth is, I want to do it all. I want to do everything, go everywhere, learn everything, experience everything, be everything. Everything that interests me, that is. And a lot of things interest me.

Part of what my mom saw when I was a kid was that while I had above-average capabilities and intelligence, I was an underachiever in school. Or rather, I was an erratic achiever. I did just fine in subjects that interested me and couldn't care less about those I didn't. This, of course, frustrated the heck out of my mother and my teachers.

Except for its social aspects, school always seemed like a colossal waste of time. Most of my real learning took place outside of school. I read voraciously, had good friends of all ages and descriptions, was a keen observer and a good listener, acquired new skills, wandered as far as my legs, and later on, my bike, would carry me, and earned money in various creative ways.

As kids, though, we're judged by our school achievements (i.e: grades) rather than those in the greater world. Because I indulged in what I wanted to do rather than in what they expected of me they thought I didn't want to do much.

The living of my life has proved them wrong. I have earned academic degrees and professional certifications and awards, and had a number of careers. And I will probably acquire and practice a few more before I quit this planet.

I love learning and becoming proficient at new skills. Then, once I've mastered and practiced them awhile, I want to learn and do something new.

I've been extremely fortunate to have traveled to a great many places in this world and hope to travel to a lot more. I'm fascinated with people and cultures.

I seem to need change, newness, variety. And I need challenges. I've often tackled a thing just to see if I could do it. I need the feeling of accomplishment when I've met the challenge. Of course, that means I've taken risks and known failure. But that doesn't keep me from continuing to seek out and take on new challenges.

People often remark, "Carol, you really are something."

My response is to laugh and say, "Yeah, but nobody's ever been able to figure out what." I say it in jest but it's true. As soon as they think they've gotten me pigeonholed I do a One-eighty and become something else.

It's also a fact that I usually do several things at once. I usually juggle at least six projects at a time, with more on the drawing board.

Not long ago, a friend, a Thai mystic, asked to see my hand. She examined my palm -- a myriad of lines going ever'-which-a-way, constantly intersecting and interrupting each other. "You don't have any choice about all the changes in your life. It's your destiny."

Well, maybe that explains it. Perhaps it's as much a part of my DNA as the color of my eyes or the shape of my toenails. And perhaps it's why I've always been drawn to the new and the different. It's my destiny.

And because of it I've had a wonderful life. Not every part of it was wonderful, but overall it's been amazing.

I was born an optimist and I'm bound to die one.

* * *

CELEBRATE THE RIDICULOUS

Sometimes life is ridiculous, and as we have progressed through it, sometimes we were ridiculous too. People may have snickered at us, and now looking back, we can laugh at ourselves as well. Celebrate the ridiculous.

Not only is it healthy to laugh at yourself, but in doing so, you make yourself much more lovable, more interesting and more real to your readers. You give them a hero to relate to and identify with.

We were all "innocents abroad" at one time. And we've all had "learning experiences" -- incidents which, although painful or embarrassing at the time, we can laugh about now.

Tragedy is something happening to you;
comedy is something happening
to someone else.
Charlie Chaplin

Here's one of my own loss-of-innocence stories. I was 19, on my way to Europe to join my Army-draftee husband in Germany. It was virtually my first foray into the world outside my San Joaquin Valley hometown.

A Hick From the Sticks

New York City's sweltering heat blasted me as I stepped out of Grand Central Station that July day in 1955. Surrounded by my mismatched luggage, I carried everything I couldn't cram into it. From one arm hung a heavy wool coat and an oversized purse. A camera and huge binoculars dangled from the opposite shoulder. With my free hand I hailed a taxicab.

A sunflower-yellow cab pulled up and stopped in front of me. The driver just sat behind the wheel looking at me, like "Ya want dis cab or not? If ya wannit, openna damn door and get in?" I opened the back door, struggled to get my heavy suitcases, huge handbag, bulky coat, binoculars and camera into the cab, climbed into the backseat and sat down, closing the door behind me. I gave him the name of my hotel and off we drove. "Where ya from?" he asked. "Yer first trip ta New Yawk?" "What're ya heah fohr?"

I answered absently, trying not to appear the proverbial hick craning to gape at the city's skyscrapers.

Once again, in front of the hotel, he just sat, making no move to get out and open my door or offer assistance with my bags, all of which was standard procedure back home.

The meter read $1.55. I handed him two one-dollar bills and held out my hand for change. His jaw dropped. I looked him steadfastly in the eye, moving my hand slightly to indicate I expected change.

"I gotta eat, lady."

I kept my hand in the same demanding position.

He dropped a nickel into it. "I got kids at home, ya know."

I just stared him in the eye, holding my open hand in his face. Continuing to plead his case, he deposited one nickel at a time until I had the full 45¢. Then I declared, self-righteous as all get-out, "A tip is for extra service, not for just doing what you're already getting paid to do."

I was downright proud of myself for not letting this city-slicker cab driver take advantage of me. In a bit of a huff I unloaded all my belongings onto the sidewalk and he drove away shaking his head.

Two days later, en route to the S.S. Hollendam for the transoceanic voyage to Rotterdam, I returned to Grand Central Station to pick up the rest of my baggage: a steamer trunk and a footlocker. The ride to the station was the same as before: no assistance from the cabbie.

I asked the driver to wait while I collected my belongings from the baggage dock. A Redcap loaded my luggage onto a cart, which he pushed through the station and out to the sidewalk. He lashed my bulky gear to the rack on the back of the cab. I handed him what I thought was a generous tip -- a couple of bucks.

He held up his hand like a cop stopping traffic, shook his head and set me straight. "The standard charge is a buck-fifty per item. Plus a tip."

"Oh." I flushed hot-flash fuschia. I have a feeling we're not in Kansas anymore, Toto.

I gave him the full amount, plus a bit more, and got into the cab. All the way through the Holland Tunnel and to the port in

New Jersey I sat in shamed silence. When we got to the Holland America pier where the Hollendam was moored, I gave this cabbie his full tip, and some extra.

Thus did I learn my first lesson in the ways of the world.

* * *

So there it is, my loss-of-innocence, coming-of-age story. Although seriously embarrassed at the time, I love this story now. I love that small-town kid's assertiveness . . . and courage . . . and her ability to laugh at herself.

That's one of the wonderful things about writing your life stories. It puts you in touch with yourself -- at all stages of your growth -- as nothing else could, and gives you a better appreciation of yourself.

WRITING ABOUT OTHERS

Throughout your life you've known a great many people, some of whom may warrant only a mention in passing, while others inspire volumes.

Your autobiography is about you, to be sure, but you'll also want to write about the people who influenced you, who inspired you, who had an impact on you -- a teacher, preacher/priest/rabbi, a neighbor, a radio or TV personality, or even a stranger who happened to do or say something that changed the way you thought or behaved. You'll want to write about your parents and grandparents, siblings, and maybe other relatives. You'll write about your best friend, your nemesis, your boss or coworkers, and many others who have crossed your path.

Unless you have lived your life in total isolation your stories about yourself will be about other people too. A lot of them may find their way into your memoirs.

In the pages that follow are tips on writing about other people and some information about the legalities.

YOUR UNIQUE RELATIONSHIPS

Your relationships with the people in your life are unique. You know different things about them than anyone else does. Your experiences with them are one-of-a-kind. They shared things with you that they've shared with no one else. They showed you a side of themselves that no one else knows. As a result, your perception of them is different than anyone else's.

Your experience of your father, for example, was different from that of your siblings. Although you had the same father, your portrayal of him may be someone your siblings barely recognize. There could be many reasons for this:

- Your personality is not the same as theirs so he did not relate to you the same as he did to them. He may have punished you differently; he may have discussed philosophy with you but not them; he may have taken your siblings to football games and left you home to shovel snow; he may have adored you and been indifferent to them; the two of you may have been on the same wave length and laughed at each other's jokes, or had nothing in common at all.

- He was at a different stage of life when you came along than when your siblings did, so his daily stresses were not the same. He may have had different health issues.

His relationship with your mother may have changed; he may even have had a different wife. His job may have been more (or less) time-consuming and/or stressful. All these things, and much more, affected his personality and temperament.

Innumerable variables make your relationship with him unique.

Every human being is so multifaceted that each person who knows him or her -- each relative, friend, neighbor, co-worker, etc. -- may know a different person who inhabits that same body.

Even if everyone else has written about a person, your knowledge of and relationship with him or her is like no other's. So go ahead, write *your* recollections. Tell *your* story.

ANECDOTES TELL THE STORY

When writing about a person, don't just gush or rant about how sweet, charitable, churlish or nasty old "So 'n' so" was. Show it with an anecdote (a short story or word-picture)) that engages the reader and demonstrates just *how* that person was sweet, charitable, churlish, or nasty.

When you write about someone, write scenes, tell tales, paint "pictures" to create an image in your readers' minds so that they can fully experience the scene and the person. An anecdote will tell far more about a person than will just a description or label.

Here's one about my Aunt Bill (Willie Katherine Hartley, 1902 - 1986):

Every year by the end of May, Aunt Bill's half-acre yard was ablaze with color; gladiolas, zinnias, asters, Shasta daisies, larkspur, delphiniums, marguerites, marigolds, stocks, and I don't know what-all.

And roses! Aunt Bill's roses always took prizes at the Fresno County Fair and Rose Society competitions. People driving by often stopped to admire the spectacular array of roses that rimmed her front yard.

Every year she worked all through the night before Memorial Day. She spent the evening picking wheelbarrows full of the flowers and greenery needed to complete her labor of love and patriotism. To keep them fresh she stood them in galvanized buckets of water. Surrounded by their fragrances, she went to work in the breezeway between house and garage making floral arrangements.

Hers were not simple homemade bouquets, nor were they skimpy. Always the artist, Aunt Bill made dozens of full-blown, elegant arrangements. As she worked she hummed or whistled.

Early on Memorial Day, someone drove her out to the Washington Colony Cemetery where she placed a bouquet in the sunken metal cylinder on the grave of every veteran. She saw to it that each soldier, sailor or marine buried there was properly honored.

When she got into her 80s, arthritis slowed her down. She swore in frustration at her stiff fingers as the bouquets painstakingly took shape. And she cussed at her creaky knees as she knelt on the graves to place her floral tribute. But she didn't quit until homage was paid to every last veteran there.

* * *

Instead on an anecdote I could have written a gusher, e.g: "My aunt was a good, kind person. You'd have liked her. She was an amazing woman, an artist and a patriot."

All that is true, but does it tell anything about her that you can grab hold of? Do you get a picture of her in your mind? Do you get any sense of who she was? If so, you have an amazing imagination, maybe even psychic powers. Most of us need more. We want examples that show how she was a good person; why we would have liked her; how she expressed patriotism.

On the other side of the coin, here's an anecdote about my stepfather, whom I will call "LT."

LT loved to goad people until they blew up. Then he smirked and boasted, "Didn't take me long to get his goat." I guess it made him feel clever or powerful.

He also thought it was funny to cause pain or trauma. And I was his favorite victim.

Back then, before TV (Fresno didn't get TV until 1953) and air conditioning, everyone spent the hot summer evenings outdoors. Huge, hard-shelled, hissing, spitting June bugs buzzed around the porch lights. LT delighted in grabbing a handful and stuffing them down my shirt. Then, while I screamed in terror and squirmed in revulsion, he threw back his head and laughed, slapping his thigh, enjoying my torment.

* * *

I could have just said LT was sadistic, which is true. But there in print is the proof. This little anecdote shows *how* he was sadistic.

Anecdotes provide the hows and the whys. They give concrete examples. "Sadistic" is nothing but a foggy concept -- a meaningless label. So are "kind," "patriotic," and "artist."

I'm sure you'll agree, it's easier to get a grasp on concrete than fog. It's your anecdotes, your concrete examples, that make the people in your stories come alive. They prove your point and make your readers love -- or hate -- the character, right along with you.

Pretend you're in a courtroom: You're the prosecutor. If you merely tell the jury that the defendant is guilty, you're going to lose. You have to give data, examples, evidence. In other words, you must prove your case.

So it is in writing. You have to convince the "judge and jury" (your readers) of the case you're making.

Don't shortchange your readers or your subjects by writing "fog." Oh, you can state the concept -- the fog: "She was a good person." Or, "He was a jerk," but then tell the anecdote that demonstrates it. Give your readers something concrete to hang onto.

IN THE BEST OF FAMILIES

So you've got weird relatives, who doesn't? Nobody's perfect. Everybody's got warts. Some people hide them better than others, but everybody's got 'em. Part of what makes people interesting and gives them character is their flaws and inconsistencies, their contradictions. So, as you're describing yourself or your other characters, give the full picture. Leave the warts in.

As the old saying goes, "It happens in the best of families."

Surely you want your readers, especially your grandchildren and great-grandchildren, to know the real you and your other honest-to-goodness real relatives. You don't want them to think you and all their other relatives were saints or angels, do you?

For instance, you may want to write about your ultra-religious grandmother, the straight-laced, proper lady whose public behavior was above reproach, the stern matriarch who viewed anything modern or fun as sinful. (That was my grandma.) Perhaps this same grandma, when she thought no one was looking, nipped at the medicinal brandy, peeked at Uncle Izzy's raunchy magazines, and swore like a tinker when the goat gobbled her sheets on the clothesline. (I don't think my grandma did any of those.)

Now, admit it, isn't that old lady a lot more interesting than when she was just a "proper lady."

Your readers, especially your family members, will be delighted to learn about your infamous relatives and friends -- the black sheep, the naughty ones, the outlaws.

And if that black sheep is you, well, isn't that why you're writing your memoirs -- to tell your side of the story? Maybe you were maligned or misunderstood. It's time to set the record straight.

The genealogy buffs in my acquaintance are delighted to find a rapscallion in the family tree. The ancestors who went about their daily life keeping their noses clean and staying out of trouble are the norm in most families. We're happy that most of our ancestors were fine upstanding people. But if everyone in the family was exceptionally virtuous it could get mighty boring. We need an occasional scalawag in the family bloodline, if only for comic relief.

Of course, one's appreciation for the family's rogues increases with time and distance. If your own parent or sibling is the rascal, your appreciation may be diminished. You may still be embarrassed or humiliated by him or her. You may continue to harbor anger or resentments toward that person. (If so, write about it.)

But by the time future generations read about the scamp the emotional baggage will be gone. They'll probably be relieved to learn that not everyone in the family was perfect. It will take the pressure off them. So, if you know some scalawag stories of your ancestors or relatives, go ahead and tell them. Your readers will love it.

I've only recently learned why my mother's family moved from Missouri to California in 1923, when Mom was 15 and her brothers Henry and Harry were 17 and 18. As the story goes, one day, the sheriff came to Grandpa and said, "Bill, if you don't get those boys of yours out of the county by morning I'm going to have to arrest 'em."

It happens in the best of families.

Grandma and Grandpa, my mom, and her teenage brothers hurriedly packed up and, by dawn the next day, were on the road to California.

Well, Mom and her siblings are gone now and no one knows the rest of the story. My cousins and I have fun conjecturing about it. My guess is that it had something to do with alcohol. It was during Prohibition and I suspect the boys were bootlegging or moon-shining.

My kids and their cousins, and their kids, all of whom are generations removed and never knew my uncles, are tickled pink to hear about them. It adds a tasty bit of spice to the family "soup."

You may not want to open the closet door too wide and reveal *all* the family skeletons, especially if someone you care about would be hurt by it. If for instance, Uncle Bud was a real louse, but Mom loved her brother and forgave him anything, you may decide to soft-pedal a bit on the subject of Uncle Bud.

If, on the other hand, Mom is no longer with us, or if Uncle Bud's "louseness" is essential to your story, you may go ahead and tell it. Or you may write about it now but not show that part to Mom. Or you may write about it and sit down and read it to her and have a long-overdue talk. (That's my recommendation.)

Only you can decide how much you are willing to censor yourself, if at all. You may simply decide to tell all and let the chips fall where they may.

QUIRKS & IDIOSYNCRASIES

Along with their flaws and inconsistencies, please write about your characters' quirks and idiosyncrasies. You may not even be aware of your own eccentric traits and mannerisms, so you probably won't write about them. But you are aware of other people's. Include them in your stories. It will make the characters more real to your readers, and much more fun.

One of the more memorable movie characters is Sally (Meg Ryan) in *When Harry Met Sally* (which has become a classic). When ordering in a restaurant she was very specific and requested some things to be served "on the side." While that may not be the thing you remember most about Sally, I'm sure you'll agree that her little idiosyncrasy in restaurant-ordering helped make her memorable.

In *As Good As It Gets*, Melvin (Jack Nicholson) was a neurotic who avoided stepping on cracks in the sidewalk, and who used a new bar of soap every time he washed his hands. Quirky, but interesting.

My little anecdote about my Aunt Bill states, " . . . as she worked she hummed or whistled."

These small touches humanize a character and make him or her more vivid in your readers' minds and experience.

YOUR MEMOIR AND THE LAW

But what if I get sued?"

This subject always comes up in my memoir classes. I've made up a handout, from which I've excerpted the following:

There are two general areas of the law that apply to your writing: defamation of character and invasion of privacy. The main things you need to know about them are:

DEFAMATION OF CHARACTER

To be ruled defamatory, a statement must be:

- False. A statement that can be proved is not defamatory.

- Published. The statement must be communicated publicly.

- Stated as fact. Statements that clearly represent an opinion are relatively safe from defamation suits.

- About a named or identifiable person. Your statement is considered defamatory only when the person is named or recognizable because of his/her personality, physical description, or other identifying characteristics.

- About a living person. Generally speaking, no one can sue you on behalf of a dead person.

- Damaging or injurious to the person concerned. For it to be defamatory, your statement must cause the person to be held in public contempt or hatred, damage his/her ability to make a living, or cause him/her to lose a spouse.

INVASION OF PRIVACY

'Invasion of Privacy" can encompass several situations that apply to a memoirist:

- The publication of offensive or embarrassing private facts about an identifiable person – facts that are not already a matter of public record.* The definition of what is embarrassing or offensive is based on the "community standards" of your locale.

- Using facts in a way that conveys a person in a false light. This is different from defamation in that here the facts are used to mislead, though they may be true.

- Using someone's name or picture for commercial gain without their consent. For example, if someone you write about in your memoir is famous or has a money-making interest in his or her name, image, etc., be very careful about using them if you plan to publish your memoir for profit. In such cases, get written permission.

That's just a quick sketch. If you have doubts or concerns, learn the laws regarding Defamation of Character and Invasion of Privacy in your state or community.

* Anything that's public record is fair game.

Writing Activity #8

Write about a person.

• Pick the person who will be your topic.

• Use the Balloon Method to remember everything you can about him or her.

• Decide what you want your reader to know about that person.

• Let your reader know about your relationship with him/her.

• Write an anecdote (or several), paint *word pictures* with *concrete examples.*

• Write about how that person influenced, inspired, impacted you and your life -- what s/he meant to you.

• Tell what was unique or unusual about him/her.

• Humanize him/her with flaws, inconsistencies, contradictions, quirks, idiosyncrasies. Leave the warts in.

• Use dialogue. Putting words in his/her mouth will give him/her character and personality.

• Have fun.

THE HARDEST PART OF WRITING

Life is not just a bowl of cherries -- sometimes it's the pits. You will do yourself and your readers a disservice if you only include the sweet parts and discard the pits.

If not for the tough times and/or the people who maligned or mistreated you, you would not be the person you are today. Adversity can strengthen a person. It can alter the course of one's life. It is often through adversity that one gains wisdom. It's been said that "Adversity is God's university." Sharing your misfortune with readers is an opportunity to pass along your hard-won wisdom.

Every film or novel worth its salt has an antagonist -- a villain or treacherous situation or condition. Set the stage, introduce the antagonist, show the steps leading to your loss, misfortune, mistreatment, humiliation, tragedy, ruination, betrayal, shock injustice. Demonstrate how you dealt with it and were transformed by it. That's the drama in your story. Note the events that were catalysts for change and your reactions, feelings and conflicts which demonstrate the growth that came about as a result of them.

Your life is determined not by what happens to you,
but by how you respond to what happens to you.

By telling about your tough times you may feel vulnerable. That's not a bad thing. If readers are going to care about you and your life you must allow them to become emotionally involved. It's largely the telling of the difficulties in your life and how you dealt with them that accomplishes that. Without emotion in your writing you're just a reporter -- a detached observer.

Frank McCourt, author of *Angela's Ashes,* said, "Telling the truth is the hardest part of writing." But that didn't keep him from doing it. *Angela's Ashes* tells of his painfully impoverished childhood, his drunken, abusive father, his disgraced, humiliated mother, and his brothers, all suffering through. He wrote about how he coped with it and how he felt about it.

Angela's Ashes won the Pulitzer Prize for Literature, stayed on the New York Times Bestsellers List for a very long time, and was made into a movie.

Why knows, maybe someday we'll see *your* story on the bestseller lists or in a movie. It may even win a Pulitzer Prize. It could happen.

Below is a poem by Sue Denim of Tuscon, AZ, demonstrating that sometimes life is the pits.

I WANT YOU TO LEAVE

I don't want to be married anymore.
Yeah, that's right. I don't.
I want you to leave. Now. Go

You look stunned. You're hurt. You're angry.
You're feeling rejected and unloved.
You're confused.

Well, turnabout's fair play, for
right after the "I do's"
you started with the "I don'ts."

"I don't love you."
"I don't want to make love to you."
"I don't care about your needs."

Why did you marry me
and bind my life to yours
only to use me and abuse me?

I thought, If only I can be perfect
-- sweet and sexy and fun --
then surely he will love me.

So I jumped through hoops to please you,
knocked myself out day by day.
You never tried to please me.

No, you ravaged me with rage,
rejection and rebuke, you
raped my soul with bogus love.

Hmmmm . . . Now you say you love me;
you cannot live without me.
That's not love. That's selfish fear.

Love is connection and caring,
support, growth and sharing.
I doubt you know how to love.

You do know how to destroy,
to disparage, diminish, disdain.
My heart is dead . . . and with it, love.

So I don't want to be married anymore.
Yeah, that's right. I don't.
I want you to leave. Now. Go.

Now I'm not angry or hurt or confused.
I'm just weary. Done in. Burnt out.
Now it's time to take care of me.

I'm going to need to rebuild myself,
to revive the parts that died.
I must relearn to love myself.

So I don't want to be married anymore.
Yeah, that's right. I don't.
I just want you to go. Now.

YOUR YELLOW-BRICK ROAD

How did you become the person you are today? As you've gone through life internal changes have occurred; changes in your world-view, changes in your character and attitude. That's what your readers want to know about. They want to follow your growth to gain insight into the person you have become.

They want to know about the incidents and situations that brought about the changes in your character, and maybe even changed the course of your life. But keep in mind, it was not the events that changed you. It was your thoughts and emotions regarding them, and your subsequent decisions and actions -- *how you responded to them*. The incident itself was neutral. It's how you felt about it and responded to it that's the story.

The situation or event is merely the hat rack on which to

hang your story. The story is *YOU*.

The classic movie, *The Wizard of Oz* is a great metaphor for life and an excellent model for an autobiography, short story or anecdote, or all of the above.

As you're constructing your story, let the reader in on:

- Your goal or objective. It may change as you go along, as Dorothy's did, but be sure the reader knows what it is.
- The start of your journey, your conflict or troublesome situation, your decision and subsequent actions.
- The turning points, roadblocks, obstacles, detours, landmarks and signposts.
- The perils and risks en route to accomplishing your goal.
- The people or elements that assisted you.
- Your arrival at your destination -- your Emerald City.
- Your thoughts, emotions and inner conflicts through the course of your journey.
- Your inner changes; how you grew in wisdom, courage, strength, confidence, compassion, maturity, *et cetera*.
- How your goal was accomplished.

Let your reader know how you traveled your own yellow-brick road to reach your own Emerald City. (This is discussed further in the section titled, "Elements of a Good Story.") This can be done in a simple anecdote or a whole book or screenplay. The following story by James Walters of Minden, NV, is a small example:

A few years ago I attended a concert by Danish-born pianist and humorist, Victor Borge. That night on stage he said that people often asked him how, at nearly 90, he could still play so well. He told them, "I don't have to think about it. My fingers know where to go."

By the time I left the concert hall his statement was forgotten. I wasn't aware that my subconscious mind had filed it away for future use.

Some time later, a year-or-so-ago, as a way of processing grief, I decided I'd learn to play the piano. I had taken lessons as a child but had resisted mightily. I simply refused to practice. Playing the same piece over and over was boring; tedious. I'd rather be out playing ball or riding my bike and would escape as soon as I could. So, as an adult, I couldn't play the piano or even read music. I'd tried to learn a few times but always gave up.

Now 64, I started again, this time determined. I knew where Middle-C was on the keyboard and on a sheet of music but was forced to locate every other note relative to it. Laboriously, note by note, I set about learning to play Beethoven's Für Elise. (I didn't want to spend time on something I didn't want to listen to.) And I practiced.

When I tired of practicing and ached to stop, Mr. Borge's voice would rise up out of my subconscious. I'd hear him say, "My fingers know where to go." And I'd wonder how many hundreds of times he had to play a piece before his fingers knew where to go. His message was this: Repetition is the key to success. So I vowed to do repetitions until my fingers knew where to go.

I played it once more. And then I played it again.

A long time after that concert, Victor Borge changed my way of thinking about playing the piano, which in turn changed my practicing habits. He provided the motivation I needed in order to persevere. Without his words echoing inside my head I surely would have given up.

I still hear them when I get bored or frustrated with a piece of music. And I still ask myself, how many hundreds of times did he have to play a piece before his fingers knew where to go?

And I play it once more. And I play it again.

I'll never be a Paderewski or a Victor Borge, but I can play Für Elise and a few other pieces well enough for my own enjoyment. And it got me through my grieving.

Let's examine this little anecdote in terms of the "yellow-brick road model" on the previous pages:

- Goals/Objectives: James Walter's desire to process grief and learn to play the piano provided his goals.
- Start of Journey: His decision to learn to play the piano.
- Roadblocks/Obstacles: His boredom, frustration and a history of quitting.
- Helper/Inspirer/Motivator: Victor Borge, through James' subconscious mind.
- Peril/Risk/Conflict: His desire to quit practicing conflicted with his desire to play the piano.
- Thoughts/Emotions: His realization that practice is the key. His determination to do repetitions until his fingers knew where to go.

- Arrival at destination: He can play the piano. His grieving is past. He is satisfied and feels the pride of accomplishment.
- Growth/Change/Transformation: His level of determination increased as did his willingness to persevere. His musical ability improved.

To repeat myself, the event itself was neutral. It was neither grief nor Mr. Borge's statement that produced the change. Everyone at that concert heard the same words, and surely there were others in the audience who were grieving, but I doubt all were similarly affected. It was the personalizing of it -- the Aha! -- the decision and the subsequent actions that brought about Walter's change and growth.

Here's one of my own stories that fits this category:

The closer I got to the age at which my parents died (38 and 44) the more keenly I felt my own mortality. Very early-on I learned that there are no guarantees in life. What if I don't live any longer than my parents did? What if I leave my kids without a mother?

Neither they nor their father knew the first thing about cooking, shopping, or keeping house. The kids had small chores such as keeping their rooms sort-of picked up, rinsing and loading their dishes in the dishwasher. Along with raking the lawn and carrying in groceries, that was about it.

By the time my mom died I was a survivor. At 16 I could cook, I could sew (I'd been the family's cook and made all my own clothes since Mom took sick when I was 14), I could do the things necessary to physical survival. I wanted to make sure my kids had survival skills in case they had to finish growing up without me.

Picking up the pace in my last year or so at Sonoma State College, I took 22 units per semester. What with commuting to and from school, sitting in class, and doing all the homework and housework, I was busy . . . and exhausted.

I called a family meeting. Steve was 15, Martin 13, and Alex 8. With the five of us around the kitchen table I began. "We're all busy. Each of us has a job. Dad's job at the newspaper. You kids all have school and homework – that's your job. It's mine too. We all work hard at our jobs, and I do all the work at home. I cook all the meals, do all the laundry and most of the cleaning, all the shopping, and so forth," I started.

"How would you feel about everyone pitching in to keep the household running?"

They wanted to know what I meant.

"We can all keep our own things picked up around the house, and do laundry when it's needed during the week. With the automatic washer and dryer, that's easy. On Saturdays we'll do the vacuuming, dusting and tidying up. And since there are five of us, how about each of us taking one night a week to fix dinner? I'll take one night, and I'll do the cooking on the weekends. You can make whatever you like. If you tell me what you need from the store before I go shopping on Saturdays, I'll get it for you. If not, you can walk down to Safeway and get it yourself.

"But we don't know how to cook."

"It's time you learned," I replied. "I'll help you. Let me know what you want to fix and I'll write out instructions if you need them. And I'll show you whatever you need to know."

My husband and the kids agreed to this new arrangement. Each one prepared dinner one night a week. Steve, the eldest, was the most adventurous and provided the greatest variety in his meals. Martin did very well too. His favorite and most frequent meal was Hot Dog Goulash. Alex knew how to make Sloppy Joes and Hot Dogs, so he fixed Sloppy Joes one week and Hot Dogs the next, and then back to Sloppy Joes. I don't remember what their dad fixed but he did his share and didn't complain.

I think they were pleased with their new skills and their contributions to the household. They did their cooking stint even if we had dinner guests on their night to cook. And they learned to operate the vacuum cleaner, dishwasher, washer and dryer.

I was enormously proud of them. This new program worked well. And my anxiety about leaving motherless children was somewhat allayed. All of them are now excellent cooks and enjoy cooking. Alex went on to become a chef extraordinaire.

In bringing your readers along with you on your own yellow-brick road you're giving your readers what they really want, which is the chance to know you.

*The man who writes about himself
and his own time is the only man
who writes about all men and
about all time.*

George Bernard Shaw

ALWAYS LEAVE 'EM WANTIN' MORE

Just because something happened doesn't mean you have to write about it. Be selective. Make sure you're telling a story, not merely making a report.

Drama is life with all the dull bits cut out.
Alfred Hitchcock

A good memoir is drama, so excise your "dull bits."

You'll probably want to do some serious editing before you go to print. As you read through what you've written, ask yourself, Am I telling too much? Will I've written hold my reader's interest?

A lot of writers, especially novices, fall in love with their own words. Whey they get something down on paper it's as if it's carved into the Rosetta Stone. It has become sacrosanct by the very act of writing it. They can't bear to let any of it go.

While it's true that you want to set the stage for the scene and paint a picture with your words, and you want to include information that will allow your readers to experience it fully, you don't want to bury them in "dull bits."

As they used to say in vaudeville, "Always leave 'em wantin' more."

The secret of being tiresome is in telling everything.
Voltaire

TRUTH IS IN THE EYE OF THE BEHOLDER

I once knew a fourth-grade teacher who arranged for an accomplice to open the door in the middle of class and release a cageful of pigeons into the classroom. You can imagine the chaos that ensued as the kids tried to catch or dodge the birds.

The purpose of this bizarre episode was to set up a writing exercise. When everything had calmed down and the birds were removed the children wrote about their experience. The event was not discussed. The kids took pencil in hand and wrote about it.

As you might imagine, each story was different. And each story was absolutely true. While it was a shared experience, it belonged uniquely to each child.

We all have our own truth. We see things from our own point of view. We react to an event in our own way.

Whatever you write, there may be someone else who will say, "That's not how it happened. Here's how it really was . . ." But that's *their* truth. You're writing *your* story: what you remember, your perceptions, what you know, what's true for you.

You are writing from *your* experience. If others disagree with you, let them write their own story.

ACCESSORIZE

In addition to writing what you remember you may want to accessorize a bit in order to paint a picture, set the scene, create the mood and invite your reader in.

It's like a woman dressing for a special event. She puts on her little black dress. It's nice but not stunning. Then she begins to accessorize. She slips on ultra-sheer black hose and high-fashion shoes, adds jewelry or a scarf, and completes the ensemble with a chic hat, gloves and bag (or parasol, as in the illustration).

The basic dress and shoes are the bare essentials. It's by adding accessories that she increases her chances of being noticed and fully appreciated.

It's the same with your story. The story's basic dress and shoes are the bare facts. As a writer you can enhance it by dressing it up. Embellishing it. You can allow your imagination to drift a bit in order to create the accessories.

When I wrote the below excerpt from an anecdote there was a lot I didn't remember. (I was only 4.) I embellished my actual recollections with some "what could have beens." The story didn't change, so it's still "memoir" rather than "fiction".

Grandma's Stereopticon

When I was a kid the only stereo system we knew about was not something you listened to, it was something you looked through. It was a wondrous contraption and it was all the entertainment my sister and I could have hoped for on a sizzling summer afternoon.

The coolest place in our central valley farmhouse was my grandmother's bedroom on the north side of the house, shaded by umbrella trees. If there was any breeze at all it came through the open windows, fluttering the lace curtains and riffling the roses in the pitcher on the washstand. The chirps and tweets of birds came in through the windows. Beneath Grandma's step-up walnut bed was a wooden box which she brought out infrequently. If it had been an everyday occurrence it would have taken away from it. No, it was special and, to us, quite magical.

One scorching day the summer Patsy turned seven and I was almost five, Grandma invited us into her room where the scents of fresh roses, lavender sachet, and Old English greeted us. She had a surprise. With smiling eyes, my tiny Danish grandmother, who smelled of Rosewater and Glycerin, knelt beside the bed, her joints stiff and her movements awkward. Carefully lifting the crocheted bedspread, she pulled out the box.

She lifted the lid and exposed its contents as if revealing Aladdin's treasure. Excitement tickled through our small bodies.

In the box were a strange apparatus, a stereopticon, and a stack of postcard-sized photographs. The stereopticon consisted of a metal eyepiece similar in shape to a snorkeling mask. Beneath it was a wooden handle and, extending out front, a wooden slider. Atop that was a wire picture holder which could be positioned for focus.

The photographs were unique as well. They were sepia-toned side-by-side twin photos, some of which were hand-painted in vibrant colors. There were photos of the boardwalk at Atlantic City, Native Americans in their tribal village, Hawaiian Islanders in grass skirts and flower leis, Victorian men and women in a "horseless carriage." And there were nature scenes: Niagara Falls, Rocky Mountain bighorn sheep, Yosemite's Half Dome.

The amazing thing about the stereopticon and its stereo-images was that when you put the pictures in and gazed through it, they sprang to life. They became three-dimensional, so real you could virtually walk into the scene. (Victorian vitrual reality!) I still don't understand how those flat photos came to life like that. All I know is that they did.

That day, after opening the box and removing its contents, Grandma actually left the room, trusting us to enjoy its wonders unattended, making us feel very grown-up and quite special. We sat on the hardwood floor of Grandma's bedroom, our bare legs grateful for its smooth coolness, and spent the afternoon engrossed in the enthralling images. The heat was forgotten. We were cooled by Niagara Falls' mist, by the wind as we raced along in the horseless carriage, by the ocean breeze in Atlantic City. . . .

To be honest, I don't remember what kind of curtains were on Grandma's window. I have no idea what kind of wood constituted her bed, or if it was the step-up kind. I don't know if there were roses on the washstand or if the box under the bed was wood or cardboard. I let my imagination wander. I asked myself, "What could have been?"

I wanted to create a scene my readers could enter and experience along with my sister and me. So I included some visual and sensory details. I wanted them to see it, feel it, smell it, hear it. Not only did accessorizing not detract from the story, I think it enriched it.

Was I lying by including details that may not have been strictly true? No, of course not. I was merely dressing up the facts to make my story more appealing to my readers.

My "what could have beens" were consistent with what I did remember and with "what probably was." We lived in a Victorian-era farmhouse filled with lovely things. If we had lived in a tar-paper shack or a palatial mansion my "what could have beens" might be inconsistent and therefore not believable.

Literary license or creative non-fiction allows a writer to take liberties in order to improve upon the story and enhance readers' enjoyment. It's still the truth. It's still what really happened. In no way is the integrity of the story compromised. It is just told in a way that is more experiential and more enjoyable.

A word of caution: If there's something in your story that is inconsistent, be sure to comment on it. If you mention the crystal chandelier in great-grandpa's log cabin, be sure to explain its presence. (That's a story in itself.) If you neglect to, your readers will be jarred by it and may even question your sanity.

Writing Activity #9

Write on any topic, employing the arts of "seduction" and "accessorizing."

• Seduction: Lead your reader on. Drop hints about things to come. Make the reader so curious about what's going to happen they'll be flippin' those pages like mad.

• Accessorizing: Embellish the details in your story. Dress it up a little to give your reader a real feed for it. Describe the setting -- paint a word picture -- using sensory devices. Make your reader smell, taste, hear, feel and see whatever is going on in the story.

• Thoughts and Feelings: Let your reader know what you were thinking and feeling. Make your reader feel something for the character(s).

Have fun.

ELEMENTS OF A GOOD STORY

What makes a good story good? What elements do your favorite books, movies and plays have in common?

For starters, let's look at the three basics of a story -- any story:

1. it has a beginning, a middle, and an end (three important events).

2. it is self-contained.

3. it has a point.

Beyond those most elementary basics of a story -- good, bad or indifferent -- let's look at the elements of a good story:

- **Introduction**: sets the stage, establishes the time and place for the action, invites the reader/viewer in. (Not necessarily in the first sentence or paragraph.)

- **Hook**: the ploy used to grab the reader's or audience's attention and get them involved. Then the writer just reels the reader into the story.

- **Sensory Descriptions**: scenes show what the characters see, hear, smell, taste, feel (tactile sensations).

- **Action**: what happens, what the characters do, say or think. Action holds the reader's interest.

- **Goal or Mission**: the hero's dream or purpose, something he or she is working toward, a feat to be accomplished. It gives meaning and purpose to the story and moves the action forward. It provides the plot.

- **Protagonist**: the hero (male or female), the good guy, the sympathetic character. In your memoir the protagonist is, of course, you. You're the one the reader relates to, sympathizes with and roots for.

- **Co-protagonist**: the hero's ally and associate, who assists, supports and accompanies the hero in accomplishing the all-important goal or mission.

- **Antagonist**: the bad guy, anti-hero, villain; someone or something which threatens the hero or obstructs the hero's mission. It can be a person or group of people, or a situation such as a storm, poverty, sickness, disability, addiction, societal scorn, *et cetera*.

- **Tension/Conflict/Struggle/Suspense**: keeps the reader turning pages.

- **Humor**: comic relief. Laughter is an important element in a story, especially to relieve built-up tension.

- **Thoughts/Emotions**: readers learn who the hero really is and how he/she is changing through his/her thoughts and feelings.

- **Transformation**: inner changes in the hero (and others) during the course of the story. The growth may be in terms of courage, inner-strength, maturity, wisdom, trustworthiness, confidence, determination, kindness, sophistication, inner-peace, self-esteem, *et cetera*.

- **Conclusion/Resolution**: the drama is resolved and the story ends.

To demonstrate these elements, let's again look at *The Wizard of Oz*:

- **Introduction:** we get acquainted with the hero, Dorothy, her family and friends, and the setting, a farm in rural Kansas.
- **Hook**: Dorothy gets hit on the head and ends up in a land of fantasy and jeopardy when things go from the familiar to the astonishing.
- **Action**: It doesn't lag. Dorothy runs away from home, then returns, gets knocked on the head, lands in OZ and spends the rest of the story in and out of peril, trying to reach the Emerald City, then completing preposterous tasks and overcoming impossible obstacles in an effort to get back home to Kansas.
- **Goal or Mission**: In the beginning, Dorothy's goal is to save her dog Toto from the clutches of meal old Miss Gulch. Once she lands in OZ, however, her overriding goal is to return to the peace and comfort of her home and family in Kansas. Her companions (co-protagonists) also have goals: a heart, a brain, courage.
- **Protagonist**: Dorothy.
- **Co-Protagonist(s)**: The Good Witch Glynda, Scarecrow, Tin Woodman, Cowardly Lion, and *The Wizard of OZ.*
- **Antagonist:** In the beginning: Miss Gulch. Then, in the Land

of OZ, the Wicked Witch of the the West.

- **Tension/Conflict/Struggle/Suspense**: Dorothy endures one perilous situation after another and we wonder how or if she's going to escape or overcome it. The witch's wickedness, one bizarre situation after another, conspire to keep Dorothy from achieving her goal.

- **Humor:** provided by the antics of the Wizard, Scarecrow, Tin Woodman, Lion, and a very cleverly written script.

- **Thoughts & Feelings**: Dorothy agonizes over her plight, expresses astonishment at the odd goings-on in the curious land, voices terror and doubt as she is tested, declares faith in her companions and the Wizard, and longs for her Kansas home.

- **Transformation**: Dorothy realizes there's no place like home, and she's always had the power to return.

- **Conclusion/Resolution**: After multiple hazards and terrors, Dorothy and her companions complete the tasks set by the Wizard; the wicked witch is dead. The Wizard himself is debunked, her companions realize they already have what they longed for, and Dorothy and Toto return home.

Although all of these elements may not be present in every good story, nearly all are found in all good stories.

As you're writing your stories you might refer back to these pages from time to time and make use of the above elements. Or, having written a story, you might check to see how many of them you've instinctively used. I think you'll be amazed to find that they're already there.

You've always had within you the power and ability to tell a really good story.

To be sure, writing autobiographically may be different from writing a novel or screenplay, so some of this may not apply to everything you write. Autobiographical writings may at times be a series of recollections, or an introspective retrospective, an essay, or any number of other things rather than a mere story.

Whenever you do write a story -- memoir or fiction -- keep these elements in mind. To be a "good read" your memoir needs to be a good story or a series of good stories, as well as whatever else you choose to include.

Writing Activity # 10

Write a story using an event as the "hat rack." Use as many of the elements in the previous section as you can. Pay special attention to "Transformation." The event can be something that made the 11 O'clock News, or one known only to you.

• Use "The Balloon Method" to help you remember every thing you can about the event.

• Show your character's motivation/goal/dream, and how he/she/you accomplished it (or failed).

• Build tension/conflict/suspense into the story.

• Transformation: Show how you and others changed over the course of the story: what you learned; how you grew.

Have fun.

Below is a story told to Ron Allen by his mother, an Irish immigrant. It holds an important place in his book of memoirs.

Please Don't Kill My Daddy!

Ronald V. Allen ~ Reno, NV

Scariff is a small village on the River Shannon. In 1917, the "Black and Tans" -- British soldiers so named for the color of their uniforms, were the occupation troops.

On a warm night in June while the curfew was in force, a donkey brayed in the night. Michael Gleeson went out the back door of his cottage at Number 7 Bridge Street and slipped along the pathway behind the row houses and found it. As quietly as he could he took the now-calm beast to a stable where there was food, water and shelter.

He was spotted by the British soldiers, though, and made a run for it.

Margaret, his daughter, who was seven years old, was terrified he would be caught. . . . or worse, shot by the soldiers. As he came in through the kitchen and then up the stairs to the bedroom, she thought of the rifle buried in the backyard. She heard her mother scold Michael for doing such a dangerous thing and was glad it was over.

Then came a shout from the street. "Come out, Gleeson. We know it was you."

Silence.

Then, finally, Michael roared from upstairs. "If it's me you want, Rigby, come and get me."

"Oh God, no!" Margaret screamed, sensing how bad the situation was.

Captain Rigby spurred his horse toward the front door and stopped with the horse's hooves on the front step, the horse and Rigby looking into the front room.

"Surround the place," he ordered. His men started to go.

Margaret was at the front door, right by the huge horse.

"Come out, Gleeson," the captain shouted.

"Never."

"Please don't kill my daddy!" pleaded little Margaret as tears wet her face.

At that moment, Rigby's eyes met Margaret's and in that fleeting instant, compassion and reason overtook conflict and rules.

"Hold it, men," commanded Rigby. The tall young British officer leaned down to the little girl, and said, "Don't cry, little one. I've a little girl just like you, and I'm not going to hurt your daddy."

He backed the horse off the step and onto the cobblestone street. As the horse turned, Captain Rigby looked back and, as if to acknowledge her courage, tipped his riding crop to his cap and rode away.

Margaret Gleeson, that little girl, was my mother.

* * *

Is there a story about one of your parents or grandparents, or someone else in your family that you could write? Your descendants will appreciate it.

BLUEPRINT FOR A GOOD STORY

There are three rules for writing the novel.
Unfortunately, no one knows what they are.

W. Somerset Maugham

It would be presumptuous for me or anyone else to say, "I have the formula for a great book or film." For whatever rule or formula one devises there are many exceptions. However, there is a formula that has worked well for many a successful novel or play.

Perhaps most of us will write only an autobiography -- a Birth-to-Present-Day chronicle -- or vignettes of the bits and pieces of our lives. For those who are a bit more ambitious, however, and wish to write a novel or play about a piece of their lives, the structure on the next page may be helpful.

Fitting your story into this structure improves it. It makes it far more exciting and turns it into a page turner. It's simple, though it may not be easy. Try it. You may end up with a bestseller, mega-movie, or Broadway play. It works well for the short story, too.

Before you start writing, give your story some thought. Picture it in terms of this structure, along with the "Elements of a Good

Story," of course. They're compatible. Map it out with this structure in mind.

Screenwriter William Goldman said, "Screenplays are structure." Period. So are novels and stage plays. The structure looks like this:

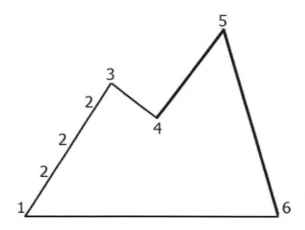

1. The inciting moment. the situation or action that gets the story going and gets the reader or audience involved. (The hook.)

2. Complications. Pile 'em on. Get your hero in a lot of trouble, them pile on some more.

3. Crisis. The situation is terrible. Tension is high.

4. Reversal. Back off a little, relieve the tension a bit, then spike it.

5. Catastrophe. Gadzooks, things can't get any worse!

6. Solution & conclusion. The problem is solved and everyone's happy (except the villain). *The End.* Roll the credits.

From now on, as you read a novel or watch a play on stage,

screen or TV, be aware of these six building blocks. See how often this structure is used to create a truly gripping story.

You may ask, what does this have to do with writing autobiographically?

It's said that all fiction is autobiographical. Every writer draws on his or her own experience, perceptions and conclusions.

Creativity is real life expanded by one's imagination. It starts with what we know, what we have experienced and observed, and extends outward. It can extend as far in any direction as you care to take it. It can be as benign or as bizarre as you wish; as sentimental or terrifying; as tame or thrilling.

Even writers like Stephen King, whose creativity and imagination seem to know no bounds, start with real life. If they didn't, readers couldn't relate to their stories and characters and their books wouldn't get read.

Use your own real life stories as your starting point and expand upon them. Use your imagination.

The blueprint on the preceding page works well for any genre: mystery, drama, comedy, adventure, horror, romance, science fiction, fantasy, children's books, and yes, memoir. Several of my memoir students have used this structure for a memoir, and a few have gone on to write novels and find this "blueprint" enormously helpful.

Writing Activity #11

Write a story using the structure on the previous pages.

- Pick a topic: a situation or event from your past.

- Use the Balloon Method to help your recall.

- Start off with a bang. Get right into the story with a grabber of an opening sentence and "the inciting moment." Lay out your hero's problem early-on -- in the first sentence, if possible.

- Demonstrate that your hero really wants to solve the problem; tell why s/he must solve it, what will happen if s/he doesn't. Make the stakes high.

- Introduce the other important characters. Give them and your hero quirks, idiosyncrasies.

- Make your antagonist as nasty/terrible as your Imagination can conjure. Remember, the antagonist can be a living thing (person, animal, alien) or a bad situation.

- Build the tension. Pile on the complications.

- Use "cliffhangers."

- Accessorize. Enhance your story -- embellish facts as necessary. Bring in sensory details (smells, tastes, sounds, sights, tactile sensations), and sixth-sensory details (intuition -- gut feelings).

- Engage the reader's emotions; reveal the hero's thoughts

and feelings.

- Seduce your reader. Hint about what's to come. (It's called "foreshadowing.")
- Hero solves the problem, story concludes.

Have fun.

THE ULTIMATE CONCLUSION

In real life things don't always get wrapped up in a neat little package with all the loose ends tied up as they do in most novels or films. Sometimes in real life the villain wins or one's goal cannot be accomplished and must be abandoned. Nevertheless, there are conclusions. And you can write about them.

There may have been times when you didn't win, when someone or something did you in and you were forced to turn In a different direction and move on. The end of one episode is the beginning of another. "When God closes a door He opens a window."

In your memoirs you can show how you dealt with your disappointment or crises. You can demonstrate how you turned things around and prevailed despite "failure." You can describe how you kept on keeping on or pivoted and started anew.

You can write about how a tragedy or failure was a blessing in disguise (if it was); how it opened the door to a new path (if it did) and how you adapted and grew because of it, or how you coped with it, and how it helped shape the person you are today.

If you are still around to read this, the ultimate conclusion hasn't happened yet. As I tell my kids, "It ain't over 'til it's over."

All kinds of wonderful things can, and I firmly believe, will, still happen.

There's bound to be at least one more chapter or story, maybe even a novel or screenplay, in your life. What it will be is up to you.

The following is an excerpt from Jeann McDuffie's memoirs, on the theme of Pets.

THE LEASH THAT MEANT GO

Jeann Olson McDuffie ~ Santa Rosa, CA

The soft brown eyes looked up, expecting my help dealing with the foreboding force within his body.

I can do nothing but stroke that great noble head as I've done countless times before . . . searching out the special spot behind his ear where the hair is puppy-soft, like goose down.

The ominous gurgling sound of his breathing. The shudders than run unchecked through his once-powerful body. And the eyes, those soft brown eyes still expecting my help. Expecting me to know without words just what he wants and needs. But this time, old friend, I cannot help.

I get his collar and leash, and his tail goes Whump against the floor. The leash means GO!

Then the blood. From deep inside it gushes from his mouth in violent spurts, forming bubbly red splotches on the gray porch.

Brilliant. Incongruously beautiful. Deadly.

Our Rebel is dying.

Pure instinct gets him to the car, but his legs fail. I lift him inside; hoping there's still a chance. Knowing there's not. Oh please!

Life leaves him in a few soft jerks of that beloved body, and final release in the soft brown eyes that, to the end, look to me for help. Not accusing, not doubting, just trusting.

Now it is I who ask for help. Help to ease the heartache of feeling this familiar tawny body so slack and lifeless against my legs.

Reb, how we'll miss you.

Back home to clean the porch. To wash and scrub and wash some more, letting the rush of water take away the crimson splashes of blood that were life -- and death -- for our Reb.

How to tell the others? I cringe at the thought of passing to the ones I love this heavy sadness.

And so, the final act of acceptance. I put away the food dish, the water dish, the blanket and the bed . . . and the leash that meant GO!

* * *

GET AN EDITOR

Every writer needs an editor. Let me repeat that.

Every writer needs an editor!

Professional writers -- even bestselling authors -- would not think of going to press without one. Novices shouldn't either.

It's always a good idea to have someone else read your work and make suggestions. We tend to develop tunnel-vision and blind spots about our own writing. When it's pointed out we smack our foreheads and say something like, "Yoicks! Why didn't I see that?" Once we're made aware it's as plain as the hair (or lack thereof) on your head. Fellow writers are best. They're also the most willing, knowing its necessity and the potential for payback.

When I have others read my work-in-progress I ask for their input and feedback. I want to know:

What did I leave out? What did I miss?

What should I have left out?

Are there inconsistencies?

Is it clearly written? (*I* know what I'm trying to say, but have I written it so that *you* know what I'm trying to say?)

I'm like the 18-wheeler drivers on the highway with their signs asking, "How am I driving?" I'm asking, "How am I writing?" And I want my editors to tell me.

I don't always follow all of their suggestions, though. And neither will you. Sometimes they just don't get it -- they're on a different wave-length or even a different planet.

While I may ultimately reject their advice, I absolutely appreciate it. I listen and seriously consider each of their suggestions. And if I decide not to use some of them, at least I've thought it through very carefully and made the decision based on what I believe will work best.

Please keep in mind that most writers are not editors. Editing is a specialized skill and a separate profession. Editors have to know about good writing, but most writers don't know about good editing. Your writing group is not your editor It provides a different, though very important, function. (And don't expect your friend who is an English teacher to be an editor. I have edited books by several English teachers and, trust me, they are not editors.)

Please self-edit before giving your work to an editor. You'll save him or her headaches and yourself money.

The following is an excerpt from Oliver Green's memoirs on Rites of Passage/a WWII experience.

Rite of Passage

Oliver Green ~ Colorado Springs, CO

I had by now become thoroughly indoctrinated in Navy tradition and wanted to do everything that would make me "Navy." If a tattoo were a part of the process, so be it.

I had three buddies, all the same age as I. We were inseparable. We discussed the business of tattoos. One main concern was whether the tattoo would be visible on our skin. All of us were black, but different shades of black.

Big Dave had red hair and a very light complexion. Bob was of mixed blood; half white and half black. Joe was a huge man. He stood 6'5" and was muscular and mean-looking. . . . He was truly the blackest man I had ever seen. Then there was Oliver who had instigated the tattoo idea.

One evening the four of us headed into town. After a few beers to strengthen our resolve we decided we'd all get the same tattoo. One more beer and the big four -- "All for one and one for all, Navy tried and true" -- swaggered off to the tattoo parlor.

It was a dingy little place. The owner did not impress us as a reputable character. Nevertheless, we made the selection and the artist began on Big Dave. We flinched, but this was our test. To our surprise the outline on Big Dave's forearm was beautiful. The artist completed the tattoo by filling in the outline with the red and green and orange colors. I was next. My tattoo application went as easy as Dave's, and Bob followed with no problem. The artist was really skilled in his craft. The four of us cheered.

Then it was Joe's turn. We all wondered if the tattoo would be seen on his black skin. Joe wanted so much to be one of the "Big Four." The artist looked at Joe's black forearm with a wry expression. He knew the results would not be to his satisfaction, but he proceeded. As he began the outline with the needle the blue ink was barely visible under the dark skin. He shook his head, adding different colors: orange, green and red. Joe was elated with what he thought he was going to have. Finally, the work was completed.

To say the least, we were proud of ourselves. We were "Navy tried and true." Traditional sailors. We strutted around with our shirtsleeves rolled up to our elbows, displaying our prized possession. Joe did have difficulty showing off his prize. He was most proud. He could be overheard at times talking to other sailors, pointing to his forearm, asking, "Can't you see it, you damn fool?!" He intimidated people into seeing what was barely visible. They would walk away shaking their heads and mumbling to themselves. They saw something because Joe said it was there. It was hilarious!

. . . Time passes and nothing stays the same. The beautiful colors on the tattoo have faded and gone, as happens to most beauty. Nothing remains now but a blurred outline, a constant reminder of the days of growing up on the naval base at St. Julien's Creek, Virginia.

* * *

GROUP DYNAMICS

Every writer needs feedback. I recommend joining or forming a class or writers group which meets regularly. I suggest that you agree to get right to work without a lot of conversation about the latest book you read or movie you attended, *et cetera*. And I recommend that you agree to check your politics at the door.

Rule #1: Start on time, and keep the critique moving. Someone has to say, "It's time to get started. Who wants to go first?" and then, when divergent conversations start up, pull the group back on focus. Someone may take a leadership role, or maybe all members will be equally committed. I cannot over-emphasize the importance of this. Many writing groups fall apart because they lose sight of their purpose. Everyone is there to get feedback on their writing and when the group devolves into a coffee klatch their needs are not being met and they stop attending.

Even a small group of two or three can be very helpful. In the group you can ask for honest and thoughtful *constructive* feedback.

In my classes and writing groups I do not allow destructive or "brutally honest" criticism; that is, criticism for the sake of criticism. I advise writing classes and groups to have some ground rules or agreements in place from the outset. For example, when critiquing one another's writing, I suggest that you make a point to accentuate the positive; to encourage and support one another.

Please be sensitive to the tender feelings of the writer, whether novice or professional. We are all sensitive and vulnerable regarding our creative efforts.

Remember, in critiquing, as in the rest of life, it's not *what* you say but *how* you say it. Try to find a gentle way to get your point across.

There's a story about Louisa May Alcott, author of *Little Women, Little Men, Jo's Boys, et al.* Both she and a college friend yearned to be writers and enrolled in writing classes. Alcott's class was supportive, encouraging and positive. Her friend's was not. In his class, blunt criticism was the rule. We all know that Alcott went on to become a very successful author. Her friend did not. He gave up and went into some other profession, feeling like a failed writer before he'd even begun.

Having said that, if your writing group is to be useful, it's important that you be open to your fellow writers' constructive suggestions.

My suggested List of Do's & Don't's:

Do:

- ask your fellow writers to tell you what they like about your story as well as what doesn't work for them, and why.
- ask them to tell you when what you've written in unclear, and what you might to to fix it.
- ask them to tell you when you are repetitive or redundant.
- ask them to tell you when you should shorten or expand your story or a part of it.
- tell them if you wish them to correct your grammar and spelling, or not.
- listen to what they have to say; they're trying to help.
- sincerely thank everyone for evaluating your work.
- realize that the final decision is yours. Their suggestions are just that -- suggestions. It is your story and the final version is up to you.

Don't:

- fall in love with your own words; you must be willing to consider changing and/or eliminating some.
- let your ego get in the way of having the best finished product possible.
- get defensive. It's counterproductive.

If you find that your needs are not being met in your group, exit gracefully and find or start a new one.

Benefits of a Writers Group -- a Win-Win

The benefits of attending a writers group are many. Among the most important is that by attending a regular meeting of writers committed to producing a written work, you are motivated to write something for every meeting. Since the expectation is that everyone will bring something they've written to every meeting, you'll put a little pressure on yourself and actually get some work done. The expectation is not that members will bring a perfect piece of writing to the meeting. Bring whatever you're working on in whatever state it's in. That's what the group is for.

I must emphasize the importance of attending regularly, whether you've gotten something written something or not. I fully realize, as your fellow writers will, that there are times when life gets in the way and it's impossible to set aside the required amount or time or to get your mind functioning creatively. Go the meeting anyway, if possible. Your fellow writers need your input on their work, and you need the stimulation and inspiration they provide.

A vital function of membership in a writers group is simply that you provide an audience for one another's writings and life experiences.

It's a win-win situation. You get your stories written and feel good about yourself. You can't lose.

Furthermore, consider the fact that writing is a solitary affair. It's lovely to get together with a group of folks who understand and can empathize and laugh with you over the challenges and situations you encounter as a writer.

In addition, many a lasting, meaningful friendship has been forged over a weekly or bi-weekly "cuppa" and the discussion of manuscripts in progress.

Writers Class/Group Methods

Writers' groups and classes operate differently.

In some, each writer makes a copy of that week's work for every other member. The members take all the writings home and evaluate them, with notes in the margins or a longer note on the back. The following week, the author reads that work aloud. Verbal response is then requested and accepted. Or the author takes home all the evaluations prepared by fellow members and reads them in solitude.

Other groups simply have each member read his or her work aloud, and the others respond on the spot.

In yet other groups only one member submits work, and the others read and critique it in advance, coming to the meeting prepared to share their thoughts with the others.

All methods are productive and useful. You may come up with another that works for your group.

I suggest limiting the length of each meeting's written offering, and deciding on a standard format, e.g: double-spaced, 12 pt. Times font, 8.5 x 11" pages.

Class or Group Size

Most people, especially beginning writers, feel less intimidated in smaller groups. In addition, since time is limited, in a small group everyone gets a chance to read his or her work and get feedback, which is why you're there, after all.

For informal over-the-kitchen-table writers groups, 3 - 5 seems the most productive.

For a writing class: whatever size the teacher and students can handle. Unless I'm doing huge workshops at a conference, I keep them to 20 or fewer participants.

Below is an autobiographical poem:

ODE TO HAIRSPRAY

Effie Marie Larsen of Burlingame, CA

In bygone times before hairspray
    every day was a bad hair day.
Every style was so damn trying
    it would have me cursin' 'n' crying.
With many a clippie and bobby pin
    each blessed day would end and begin.
Rinses of vinegar, milk, even beer,
    they did no good, not even near.

Big silken scarves protecting our curls
    from damp fog and windy swirls
covered the heads of all of us girls,
    en route to school, jobs and social whirls.
Late in the '50s there came a strange style
    of hair up in rollers 'most all of the while,
for shopping, appointments and PTA meetings,
    so later on hubby'd bestow loving greetings.

This limp, wispy hair -- my bane of existence!
    How I prayed with impassioned insistence
for deliverance, for divine intervention,
    when Hallelujah! there was an invention.

It came in a spray can for swift application

    and changed women's lives all over the nation.

We comb, spray and run, out the door in a jiffy,

    each hair in place, curled, fluffed and spiffy.

In my book, hairspray is as much of a boon

    as penicillin, PCs, and trips to the moon.

Now nary a day goes by I don't bless

    the inventor of hairspray -- a woman, I'd guess.

READING ALOUD ALLOWED

Not only is reading aloud allowed, it's downright essential. Whether or not you're in a writers group, make it a practice to read what you've written out loud. It's an excellent method of self-editing, once you know what to look for. By vocalizing it, using two senses rather than one, you'll have a greater chance of catching errors, and you'll be better able to hear how it works in general.

It's best to read your work to someone else, if possible. When you have an audience your critical senses become more acute. And you may elicit suggestions from your listener, as well.

Although you may think you are imposing upon your friends, chances are excellent that they will be honored and delighted to listen to your life's adventures. They'll be amazed to learn things about you that they never imagined.

WILL IT SURVIVE TECHNOLOGY?

Why not just electronically record your life stories? Telling them into a tape recorder or camcorder is wonderful and I heartily recommend it, but only in addition to getting it in writing.

Tapes and CDs or DVDs wear out, fade, break, or otherwise self-destruct. Also, in this era of speed-of-light technological advancement, I can't help wondering how long the instruments on which we play the current types of audio cassettes, videos, CDs and DVDs will be available. Your descendants may end up with a bunch of recorded memoirs that are useless because they can no longer listen to or watch them.

Think, for example, of vinyl phonograph records, 8-track tapes or Beta videos. It is virtually impossible to find an instrument on which to play them, or, if you are lucky enough to get one, to find someone who can repair and maintain it. If your memoirs were recorded on them, think of the challenge it would present to someone a couple of generations from now, just to try to listen to or view them. The same sort of difficulty is probable with our current recording methods.

Imagine that you are placing your recorded or filmed memoirs in a time capsule, to be opened 50 or 100 years from now. Imagine the frustration when someone opens it and realizes that a priceless treasure has been unearthed but there is no way to access it.

If you do record your stories on audio or video devices, be sure to transfer them onto the latest technology every time it changes. If your home movies are on videos, transfer them onto DVDs now. And when the next generation of technology arrives, have them transferred again, from DVD to whatever that is. Better safe than sorry.

In my opinion, the written word has a far greater chance of surviving the ages and technological advancements. I doubt that the written word will ever go out of style. So I hope you'll take the time -- or get someone else to -- to put your memoirs in writing, thereby leaving the in a form that will survive not only the ravages of time but all of technology.

If you're using a computer I'm sure I don't need to tell you to save, save, save, and back everything up at the end of every writing session. My advice:

In case of flood, fire or pestilence, make multiple printed copies of everything and keep them in at least two different locations.

Writing Activity #12

Write about a turning point in your life; an event or on-going situation which caused you to change your life's course.

Write about:

- Your moment of truth:
- Tell about the series of events that let up to it.
- If other people were involved, tell about them and their part in it.
- What was the "last straw" -- the final thing that forced or motivated you to change course?
- Your Aha! moment that let you know things could be different.
- How it changed your life:
- Your decision and the actions you took.
- The results: where/who you are now because of it.
- Paint word pictures:
- Bring in the five senses.
- Answer the 6 W's:
* Why, What, Where, When, Why and How.

Have fun.

TIME'S A-WASTIN'

Tick tock . . .

Tick tock . . .

Tick tock.

Time's a-wastin'.

So just do it. Just get started . . . and just get it done. Take the time to write your own life's story. You'll be glad you did. And so will those who love you -- those who know you in the here and now and those who will come to know and love you through your memoir.

Tick tock . . .

Tick tock . . .

Tick tock.

MORE
WRITING
ACTIVITIES

Writing Activity # 13

Write a story in which your career or a job is featured.

Write about:

- your brilliant career
- your best/worst job
- your weirdest job
- your most rewarding job
- your most punishing job
- your first job

Tell how you got into that line of work or how you got that particular job.

Show anecdotally why it was the best (worst, weirdest, etc.) job you ever had.

Have fun!

Writing Activity #14

Write your love story.

Write about:

- how you met the love of your life
- what made him/her stand out from the crowd
- the courtship
- endearing habits, traits, mannerisms of your love
- less than endearing habits, traits, mannerisms.......
- difficulties or challenges you faced
- how your families & friends felt about your relationship
- the outcome: short-term & long-term

Have fun!

Writing Activity # 15

Write a story about the best/worst advice you ever got:

- the circumstances in which it was given
- the person who gave it to you:
- your relationship
- how/why he/she gave it to you
- your decision to heed the advice, or not
- your subsequent actions
- difficulties or challenges you experienced because of them
- other people who were affected by it
- how they felt and reacted
- the outcome – how your life was affected by it
- short-term and long-term

Have fun!

Writing Activity # 16

Write a story about synchronicity and/or serendipity (a coincidence bordering on the miraculous and/or an unexpected happy occurrence).

We all have had amazing, unexplainable, paradoxical happenings in our lives that leave us scratching our heads and wondering about the nature of the universe.

Write about one of those happenings. Be sure to include all the mystery, the wonder, the awe of it.

Use the appropriate techniques from *Your Legacy* to make your story engaging.

Have fun!

Writing Activity # 17

Write about how your life has turned out different than you'd expected. This could be from the perspective of yourself at any stage of life.

Tell what you expected – and what you got.

Write your emotions: bewilderment, confusion, anger, disappointment, delight, surprise, fulfillment.

Have fun!

p.s. My favorite quote, by Maya Angelou, is on the back of my memoir, *That's Life; Many Mini-Memoirs:*

Life may not be the party we expected,
but as long as we're here
we might as well dance.

Writing Activity #18

Write about your spiritual journey -- what you want known about your values and beliefs.

Write about your beliefs:

- Where you started (your parents' religion or belief system).
- What happened to change or reinforce that.
- Your "Aha!s"
- People who influenced your beliefs, one way or another.
- Religious affiliations, if any.
- Be an anecdotal as you can.
- Tell what you believe about the nature of God and/ or the universe. Be specific.

Have fun!

This is known as an "ethical will", a tradition of long standing in both the Jewish and the Chinese culture. Ethical wills have become quite common in recent years in our own culture as well. It may be the most important part of your memoirs.

ADDENDUM

The remainder of the book is a selection of mini-memoirs written by my students and friends (and one of mine). I'm including them to provide inspiration for your own stories. There may be something in them that will remind you of something you can write about.

I've published my own memoirs, *That's Life: Many Mini-Memoirs*, for the same reason. It's available at:

www.tinyurl.com/thatslife

MINI-MEMOIRS

The Imwalle House

by Mary Madsen Hallock, Santa Rosa, CA

Spring Street was not as fancy as McDonald Avenue, one block over, but it was a very nice neighborhood. Both streets were paved all the way from Fourth Street to one block shy of the rural cemetery. That last block, where the Presbyterian church is now, was a big vacant lot shaded with elm trees. Every summer a huge tent was pitched under the trees and the "Holy Rollers" held a camp meeting there. From our house we could hear them singing hymns and clapping in time to the music. That lot was at the edge of town. Beyond it were prune orchards and the countryside.

The cross streets, 13th, 14th, 15th and 16th, were not paved. A horse and wagon went up and down them delivering ice once or twice a week. Mother had a red card she put in the window if we needed ice. The position of the card indicated how many pounds she wanted, and the ice man would use his tongs to carry the right-sized chunk and put it into our icebox on the screened back porch.

Mr. Imwalle plied a route through the neighborhood, too, with a wagon filled with the vegetables he raised on his farm out west of town. He'd drive by slowly, shouting, "Wedge-tobbles," and the ladies would come out and buy from him.

Our block had an alley through its center, parallel to McDonald and Spring, with all the barns and back yards opening onto the alleys. Every morning, after the husbands went off to work, the housewives on Spring and McDonald would trot up and down the alleys, having coffee at each other's house.

One day, according to my father, Mr. Imwalle hitched his horse and vegetable wagon to the rail in front of the Exchange Bank and went inside to ask Mr. LeBaron about a large house on McDonald Avenue that was for sale.

"I'm afraid it's more than you can afford," Mr. LeBaron said kindly. "It's twelve hundred dollars."

Mr. Imwalle didn't answer. He just turned on his heel and left. But he returned immediately with two heavy buckets which he placed on Mr. LeBaron's desk.

"If dot's not enough I got two more oudt in der vagon," he said. The buckets were filled with gold coins.

When the Imwalles moved into their new house, the ladies of McDonald Avenue were all a-twitter about whether or not to call on the wife of their "wedge-tobble" man. They did, of course. And the house is still known as The Imwalle House, at least to us old-timers.

* * *

Americans Don't Ride Bikes

Ed Alterman ~ Palm Springs, CA

Bicycles were available at our hotel in the south China city of Tai Shan and we wanted to take them out for a ride. Bikes were the standard form of transportation in China and we wanted to experience the area as the locals did. Everybody rides bikes. In 1980 in China, even in big cities, the ratio of bikes to cars was at least 1000 to 1. Probably more.

We'd been assigned two tour guides, "Old Mr. Lee" and "Young Mr. Lee," who were our constant companions. They were with us ostensibly for our protection and assistance, and their approval was necessary for everything we did.

We were the first non-Chinese to visit that part of China in more than thirty years, after Chairman Mao's long reign which started with the expulsion of all foreigners, and were mobbed by locals everywhere we went. They were not unfriendly, just extremely curious about the strange creatures from afar. They had some strange notions about us.

As I said, we wanted to go biking in the countryside in and around Tai Shan, but the Misters Lee refused.

"Why?"

"Americans don't ride bikes."

"What? Why would you think that?"

"Americans all drive cars. Can't ride bikes."

"Of course we ride bikes," we insisted. "And we want to. Today!"

The Misters Lee were certain bike-riding Americans would cause accidents on the city streets and country roads. At our insistence we were finally allowed to prove our competence. We were to ride around the small lake behind our hotel, on an off-road walking path, twice without incident. Only then would we be allowed out on the streets and roads. We had no choice but to comply. They watched closely as we pedaled twice around the lake. Though disinclined, they gave their reluctant approval.

As it turned out, they were right about the accidents. We did cause a bunch of them. The good people of Tai Shan, riding their bicycles to and from work, to and from the market, to and from school, to and from business and medical appointments, were so amazed to see non-Chinese folks on bikes that they forgot to look where they were going. There was chaos at every corner as they ran into each other left and right.

We decided that the real reason our guides didn't want us riding bikes was that we'd be more difficult to control if we were to travel in any way other than en masse in the China Tourism Office's minibus.

And it's true. Once we had wheels, the ten of us scattered in nearly as many directions. Off sight-seeing individually, away from the watchful eyes of the ever-present Misters Lee, we enjoyed ourselves more than any other time on the trip, like kids let out of school.

* * *

It's Time We Danced

Bruce L. Allen, Petaluma, CA

My father's background was Baptist, but he did not tolerate what he considered the narrowness of many of the church's positions. Even so, his early religious training stopped him from learning to dance.

On the other side was my mother who was a bit of an Irish colleen when it came to dancing. She had been trained as a young girl to do Irish step-dancing and loved it. No matter how much she prodded he would not let her teach him to dance, nor would he even step one foot inside a dance hall. He thought the matter was closed.

There was a woman, however, a close friend of my mother's, named Ethel, who was a war widow at the age of 28. Ethel went to all the local dances. She fueled my mother's dreams over a cup of morning tea as she related her dancing nights.

The dancing/anti-dancing scrimmage was on, my father saying No, and my mother trying to convince him to say Yes.

In a good strategic move my mother announced that if he would not go she would go with her friend Ethel. He could drive them to the dance and pick them up later to take them home.

Now, my mother was a fine-looking woman and a good dancer. Within the first hour she was dancing every dance. Ethel came to my mother and whispered, "Did you know that Bob is standing 'way over there in the back corner? He looks so sad and alone."

The three-piece orchestra began a slow dance, Irving Berlin's *Always*. My mother started across the dance floor heading for the corner where my father stood. Several young guys approached her, asking her to dance. She declined, still walking toward my father.

She stood before him and smiled, made a little Irish curtsey, and said, "Come, Bob. It's time we danced."

My father became a dancing man that night ... and for the rest of his life ... Ballroom, Latin, Exhibition, Square Dancing ... my parents did it all!

One of my most poignant memories was my parents dancing to *Always* at their 50th wedding anniversary party.

I'll Never Drive in L.A.

Leta Inlow Fairfield Wright ~ Fresno, CA

It was World War II. America was fighting on two fronts. There was anguish in our hearts as we watched our young men and women march off to war. Americans at home pulled together in the war effort.

(My husband) Lawrence got a job designing airplanes at Lockheed, so we moved to Southern California. He was exempt from military duty because his job was vital to the war effort. We rented a little house in Burbank near the Lockheed plant. When we got there and I saw the traffic I swore I'd never drive in Los Angeles. There were so many cars and the drivers were so wild.

As the war went on, more of the men went into the military. There was a wartime song that went like this: "They're either too young or too old." Well, it was right-on. But young or old everyone did their utmost to help so that our "Yanks" over there would have what they needed.

Remember "Rosie the Riveter?" That's what we women who went to work in the nation's shipyards and aircraft factories were called. I got a job at Lockheed as a welder on the tailpipe assembly of the B -17 Flying Fortress.

I wore a metal face-shield to protect my face and eyes, and we had to wear a cover over our hair. One day a spark hit my turban and ignited my hair. I was not aware of it until my fellow workers started slapping my head to put out the fire. When it was finally out my group leader made me go right back to work. He said, "If you stop to think about it you'll be afraid to weld again." I admit, it shook me up a little.

I worked at Lockheed until Lawrence was transferred to Phoenix on temporary assignment. That's where Charlie, who was 5, got infantile paralysis.

At that time the only thing you could do for polio was the Sister Kenny Treatment: I'd soak pieces of wool blanket in boiling water. Then, picking up one with a stick, I'd put it through the wringer three times to take out the excess water and cool it off enough so it wouldn't scald him. I'd wrap each part of his body in the steaming wool, wrap that in oiled silk, then cover him with a blanket to hold in the heat. By the time one application was finished it was time to start all over again. That's how we spent every day.

After awhile we moved back to Burbank. Once a week Charlie had to go to Children's Hospital in Beverly Hills. I was determined that he would not end up crippled or in an iron lung. So, scared as I was to get on those roads with those crazy drivers, I drove him to Beverly Hills to see the doctors at Children's every week.

When the war was over we mourned for those who did not return and rejoiced with those who did. We moved back home to Fresno and resumed our peacetime lives.

Charlie had a full recovery. He is now a retired schoolteacher and has given me five beautiful granddaughters.

I Was A Kid in the War Years

Carol Petersen Purroy ~ Reno, Nevada

Fresno was the site of three military bases -- two Army and one Army Air Corps, so we were very aware of the war and the war effort. My mom and aunt both volunteered their time and effort after work and on weekends. They helped staff the Lutheran Service Center down on Broadway. Each denomination had a place where servicemen could hang out. Coffee, cookies and doughnuts were served, and there was music, ping pong tables and games of all sorts. People of all ages, including kids, did their part.

Servicemen from The Fairgrounds, where Mom had a job in the Motor Pool, were often guests in our home. They played the piano, jitterbugged with my teenaged cousin Virginia and her friends; we made popcorn or fudge, and they played Checkers or Old Maid with my sister and me.

On holidays there were as many servicemen as we could fit around the table. We'd string together the dining table with the kitchen table and a card table or two, stretching from the dining room all the way through the living room, using chairs borrowed from the neighbors and the piano bench to seat everyone.

Rationing was in effect, so we scrimped for weeks and saved up ration stamps for holiday feasts. And many things were in short supply. It was not unusual to see long lines for this thing or that. Nylons were the #1 hot item, but even things like toilet paper caused lines to form.

Franklin Delano Roosevelt was the only president I'd ever known. He'd been president since before I was born. To everyone we knew, he was some sort of god. Everyone would gather around the radio to listen to his "Fireside Chats," hanging onto his every word.

On April 12, 1945, a 6th grade girl came into my 4th grade classroom and handed my teacher, Mrs. Shirley Ludecke, a note. She signed it and the girl left. Mrs Ludecke sat at her desk and wept. We watched and wondered, but she said nothing. It wasn't until after school that we learned what it was all about.

It was at the corner store, where we sometimes stopped for a penny candy, that we got the news. President Roosevelt was dead.

The nation went into mourning and panic. The war was still on and most doubted that our new president, Harry S. Truman, was capable of leading the country. A great deal of hand-wringing went on. What was to happen to us now?

Then, within a few weeks, the war on both fronts was brought to conclusion. "Give 'em hell Harry" had what it took after all.

On VE (Victory in Europe) Day (May 8, 1945), and VJ (Victory over Japan) Day (August 15), the whole country exploded with joy and celebration.

Do It Again

Ronald V. Allen, Reno, NV

Pa bought a GMC truck for hauling wood. The truck was unusual because it had no battery. It wasn't missing; it hadn't been equipped with one. It had large magneto coils and had to be started by hand-cranking. It was a 4-cylinder. I remember the putt-putt sound it made. On very cold mornings Pa would get the truck running and then help the neighbors jumpstart their cars.

Anyway, Pa got a 3 X 8' piece of sheet steel, which he bolted onto the front of the GMC for a snowplow. Since the sheet was flat, the angle of the plow did not curl the snow off to the side as snowplows do. Instead, the force of the snow would cause the truck to slide off to one side when Pa hit the snow bank. That didn't stop him.

"We need more weight in the truck," he'd say. All the kids in the neighborhood jumped in the back. Pa then backed up the truck and made a run at the snow. When the flat sheet of steel smashed against the snow a gorgeous white plume shot 20' straight up in the air. He was having the time of his life, and so were we.

"Do it again!" we yelled. "Do it again!"

"Hang on!" he yelled back, and we waited for the resounding boom and the snow flying into the sky. He battered his way to Washington Street with all of us hanging on for dear life, beside ourselves with the joy of participating in Pa Allen's most magnificent experiment.

The Lottery Ticket

Carol Petersen Purroy, Reno, NV

The payoff for that week's California lottery was the biggest in history - $126 million! ... I couldn't help fantasizing. What couldn't I do with $126 million!

At the last minute I couldn't not do it. I raced the six or seven miles to St. Francis Shopping Center in Santa Rosa. A lot of other people had the same idea. At Safeway I waited in the long line and forked over $5 for five tickets, printed on a single slip of paper. I went back to the home in Oakmont where I was house- and dog-sitting: two adorable, frenetic Schnauzers, "Ruff" and "Tuff".

I was doing a lot of house and/or pet sitting at that time. I'd do just about anything to get away from the 10 x 12' room where I lived, in someone else's house. And, make no mistake, it *was* her house. When she was home I had to stay in my room and keep quiet. If I was cooking when she got home I had to stop immediately and turn her kitchen over to her. If I talked on the phone or played my TV (in my room) she complained because it disturbed her quietude. My friends couldn't come to the door to pick me up; I had to meet them at the corner. But I digress...

When I got back from Safeway, I carefully placed my glasses on top of the Lotto ticket at the center of the coffee table and turned on the TV. I'd be ready at 8 o'clock, in just a couple of minutes, when the winning number was announced. I wouldn't have to spend time looking for my glasses or the ticket. I turned away, probably to visit the bathroom, and got back just in time.

As the first numbered Lotto ball burst from the pack, bouncing a couple of times before coming to rest, I sat on the edge of my seat and reached for my glasses without taking my eyes off the TV. My hand came up empty. They weren't there. Frantically, I looked for the lottery ticket. It was gone too.

The dogs must've jumped onto the coffee table and snatched 'em.

I searched like a maniac. The glassed, chewed askew, I found under the couch. The third numbered ball was selected. I'd missed #2. I continued hunting. Ball #4 jumped out. I put on my mangled glasses and tore the living room apart looking for the ticket. Cushions flew off the couch. The dogs thought I was playing and got into the spirit, leaping and pouncing, treating them like toys. Ball #5 separated itself from the pack. And finally, #6.

The complete array of six numbers showed on the screen. I grabbed a pencil off the kitchen counter and scribbled them on a scrap of paper, just in case.

I scoured the house but never did find that lottery ticket. It had simply disappeared. The only place it could be was in the gullet of one of the dogs. What if I'd won the biggest lottery in California's history but my ticket in inside a dog?!

Should I take the little darlings to the vet? I couldn't know which dog had swallowed it, so they'd both have to be opened up. But they weren't my dogs. Did I have tthat right?

For $126 million, who cares?! I'd buy them new dogs.

I'd wait. If the winning ticked was purchased at Safeway in St. Francis' Shopping Center, and if no one claimed the prize, I'd take them to the vet. But, by then, would the numbers be readable? Or would the ticket be digested?

Oh, how I hated those Schnauzers!

On the 11 o'clock news, the store that sold the winning ticket was announced. It wasn't St. Francis' Safeway. I could relax. I could stop hating the dogs. And I could go to bed, my dismal financial situation unchanged.

Rats!

If you'd like to read more of Purroy's life stories, please go to:

www.tinyurl.com/thatslife

Other books by Carol Purroy:

- *MISS ROGERS STINKS* -- a historical novel, set in 1946, for 3rd - 6th grade children.
- *THAT'S LIFE; Many Mini-Memoirs* -- some of her life stories, written and published to inspire others to write their own.
- *YOUR ETHICAL WILL & TESTAMENT.* How and why to write about your beliefs and values.
- AFFIRMATIONS 101; *Survival Kit for Teens & Young Adults* (The first in a series.)

Novels by her alter-ego, "Francie Forsythe:"

- *TIARA* - Mainstream; Young Adult.

Tiara undergoes a torturous odyssey to find her true identity.

- *THE GENUINE ARTICLE* -- Mainstream; Romance; Adventure.

A tale of bittersweet revenge. Ashleigh Alexander, of Boston, sets a course for herself that takes her back to Singapore to right a wrong. In the process she threatens to sabotage her true love, destroy her fantastic career, and bring about her own destruction.

ACKNOWLEDGEMENTS

With enormous gratitude I acknowledge my editors (in alphabetical order) for their invaluable encouragement, suggestions and corrections:

Bruce L. Allen
Ronald V. Allen
Lawrence E. Green
Mary Madsen Hallock

Carol McConkie

And to those who so graciously contributed autobiographical excerpts:

Bruce L. Allen
Ronald V Allen
Ed Alterman
Freddie Mae Baxter (Knopf Publishing)
Sue Denim
Oliver Green
Mary Madsen Hallock
Will James (Scribner & Sons)
Barbara Jordan (Knopf Publishing)
Effie Marie Larsen
Jeann Olson McDuffie
James Walters
Leta Inlow Fairfield Wright

ABOUT THE AUTHOR

Carol Purroy has taught writing -- memoir, creative, and ethical wills -- at colleges, church groups, senior centers, etc., since 1991, inspiring and helping hundreds of people of all ages to write their life stories.

She was editor and publisher of senior magazines - both print and eZines. The National Association of Professional Women named her Woman of the Year in Publishing (2010), and she's listed in the *National Registry of Who's Who*. She produced and hosted TV shows, among them: *Author! Author!* and *Living Treasures*. She founded *Writers of the Purple Sage Publishing Consortium* and *Nevada Storytellers Network,* through which she co-produced a storytelling festival. She does public speaking and leads seminars and retreats.

She's traveled the world and lived abroad, and, throughout the years, enjoyed diverse careers.

A mom and grandma, she enjoys bicycle-built-for-twoing, cooking, knitting, volunteering, writing, teaching/mentoring, traveling, and gardening. She lives in Reno, Nevada.

54749708R00119

Made in the USA
Columbia, SC
05 April 2019